Life Planning in New Mexico

Your guide to state law on powers of attorney, right to die, nursing home benefits, wills, trusts and probate

Merri Rudd

❖Abogada Press
Albuquerque, New Mexico

Published by: ❖Abogada Press
P.O. Box 36011
Albuquerque, New Mexico 87176-6011
www.abogadapress.com

Copyright © 1992-2000, 2004 by Merri Rudd
Fourth Edition, First Printing 2004
Printed in the United States of America

Cover design by Carolyn Johnson

Text design by Mark Justice Hinton

Library of Congress Catalog Card Number: 92-70603

ISBN 0-9632173-8-0

This book is printed on recycled paper.

In memory of my grandmother
GRACE TUCKER
June 1, 1903-August 3, 1991

and in honor of my clients
who asked so many questions
that I had to write this book.

CONTENTS

v

PREFACE

Elder law is an area of the law that focuses on the needs of senior citizens. Many national books have been written on wills and trusts, the right to die, planning for nursing home care and other topics. To my knowledge no one has written a book to provide information on **New Mexico** law in these areas. When I represented senior citizens, I noticed that my clients were intelligent people who wished to be informed and educated about issues concerning them. Much of the information included in this book also applies to younger people.

The book will attempt to provide a detailed summary of New Mexico law that relates to seniors, their families and life planning. The book should provide enough information for people to decide what documents or planning they need or want. The book should also help people feel knowledgeable and organized if they seek the help of an attorney. While the book attempts to answer questions about New Mexico law and provide accurate information, the book is **not** a how-to-do-everything-yourself book

Anyone is free to prepare legal documents for his or her own use, but New Mexico law prohibits people who are not lawyers from preparing documents for others. Because every person's legal needs vary and because there is no way to monitor how this book will be used, I have provided only a few fill-in-the-blank legal documents.

Elder law issues are sometimes quite complex, and easy answers do not always surface. Individuals and their attorneys must reflect on death and dying, illness, family relationships, aging and other issues. Some individuals may be in the advanced stages of Alzheimer's disease and unable to answer even the most simple questions. Others may be bedridden or hospitalized with terminal diseases; these people want an attorney to help them put their affairs in order. Yet others may be active, creative people who make the aging process seem fun. I hope that people never become ill enough to have to use the advance health care directives, powers of attorney or other documents they create. But I believe that if people must encounter disaster in their lives, they might as well be prepared.

This book focuses on planning for three situations. Chapters discuss problems and rights of people who are (1) sick and incapacitated, (2) seriously ill and close to death, and (3) dying or dead. Some overlap of topics and laws may occur.

ACKNOWLEDGMENTS

Many people helped make this book better than it began. The people acknowledged here offered substantive changes, legal advice, technical advice, editing suggestions and moral support. I would like to thank Meg Adams-Cameron, Frances Andazola, Larry Durwood Ball, Bob Bustos, Claire Cumbie-Drake, Carroll Curb, Robert C. Eaton, Lori Frank, Ruben Gallegos, Tony Garcia, Sandy Giles, Charles Glass, Mary Ann Green, Tom Hall, Randolph L. Hamblin, Mark Justice Hinton (my lifeline and then some), Wilma Jensen, Carolyn Johnson, Gail Joralemon, Liz Kobel, Pam Lambert, Ellen Leitzer, Lois Long, Gaelle McConnell, Michael C. Parks, James L. Pierson, Jr., Edward J. Roibal, Judith D. Schrandt, Robert L. Schwartz, Robert Sloan, Thomas Smidt II, Forrest Smith, Mary Helen Smith, Patricia McEnearney Stelzner, Eileen Sullivan, Susan Sullivan, Susan Tomita, Patricia Tucker, Martha Wylie, Judith Zabel, the State Bar of New Mexico's Lawyer Referral for the Elderly Project, Business Graphics and my parents Irene and Irving Rudd, without whom this book never would have been written, at least by me.

1

MANAGEMENT DURING ILLNESS OR INCAPACITY

Many people fear that if they become incapacitated, no one will be able to make health care or financial decisions for them. Who will authorize the doctor to perform medical treatment or surgery? Who will decide where an incapacitated person will live? Who will pay the bills and file the Medicare or health insurance claims? Who will roll over bank certificates of deposit and handle other financial matters?

To plan ahead for possible illness or incapacity, people create documents, such as powers of attorney, that authorize another person to make health care decisions and manage their financial affairs. If someone becomes incapacitated and has not created any management documents, a court proceeding called a guardianship and conservatorship may be necessary. Alternative management methods include trusts, discussed in detail in Chapter Five, and representative payees, to whom Social Security or Veteran's Administration benefits can be paid. This chapter will discuss powers of attorney, guardianships and conservatorships in depth and will discuss briefly trusts and representative payees.

Powers of Attorney

A **power of attorney** is a legal document in which one person (the **principal**) gives another person (the **agent** or **attorney-in-fact**) or legal authority to act on the principal's behalf. A power of attorney is useful if you are ill or incapacitated, out of town or immobile. New Mexico law allows competent individuals to create a power of attorney.[1] Principals must understand what they are signing and should trust the people they are naming as their agents.

Even though a principal gives a power of attorney to an agent, the principal still retains the legal right to make his or her own health care and financial decisions. Both the agent and the principal have the power to make health care or financial decisions. If the principal were making inappropriate decisions, a guardianship or conservatorship might be necessary.

Mentally incompetent individuals cannot make powers of attorney. Those who do not know who they are, where they are, what day it is or what the power of attorney does cannot sign a power of attorney.[2] For those who are mentally incompetent and have not signed a **financial** power of attorney while still competent, a conservatorship proceeding in court would probably be necessary to provide management over their **financial affairs**.

For those who are mentally incompetent and have not signed a **health care** power of attorney while still competent, a recent New Mexico law provides for a surrogate[3] to make **health care decisions** without any writing. In disputed cases, a guardianship proceeding in court might be necessary. (Guardianships and conservatorships are discussed in detail beginning on page 22.)

New Mexico Law

New Mexico law (see page 7) provides a do-it-yourself power of attorney form with a list of powers to consider giving the agent.

---

[1]New Mexico's laws on powers of attorney appear in the New Mexico Statutes Annotated, Sections 45-5-501 through 45-5-502 and Sections 45-5-601 through 45-5-617. These statutes are available at the University of New Mexico School of Law Library (Albuquerque), the New Mexico Supreme Court Library (Santa Fe), the New Mexico State University Library located in Branson Hall (Las Cruces) and at various attorneys' offices. You may also purchase copies of these statutes directly from the New Mexico Compilation Commission, PO Box 15549, Santa Fe NM 87506; (505) 827-4821.

[2]While a person may be physically capable of signing the power of attorney, the power of attorney would not be valid.

[3]Surrogates are discussed in depth in Chapter Two.

For many years powers of attorney addressed only financial and money matters. The New Mexico do-it-yourself power of attorney form includes both financial and health care decisions in the powers given to an agent.

New Mexico law does not require a power of attorney to be witnessed. However, to be valid, a power of attorney for financial matters **must** be signed by the principal **in the presence of a notary public**[4] who notarizes the document. Technically, the notary is not a witness but is only certifying the signature of the principal. The notary public law is discussed in detail on page 116.

A power of attorney for health care matters does not require witnesses or a notary's signature. Health care powers of attorney are discussed in more detail beginning on page 9.

All powers of attorney end when the principal dies. Many people think that a power of attorney stays in effect after the principal dies and can be used to transfer property and avoid probate. **This is untrue!** An agent who uses a power of attorney when the agent **knows** the principal has died could be sued for fraud or misrepresentation. After the principal dies, the powers of the agent end. After a principal's death, the personal representative named in a will or trustee named in a trust would handle the financial affairs and distribution of the assets of the principal. Chapter Four discusses wills in detail and Chapter Five discusses trusts.

Who Should Be My Agent?

You may choose anyone you want to be your agent. Often spouses appoint each other as their agent and a trusted child as a

---

[4]New Mexico law governs how much a notary can charge for notarizing a document. For each seal or stamp the notary puts on a document, the notary can charge $5.00. Many notaries do not charge at all, especially if they work at a bank, insurance company or other business. If a notary asks for more than $5.00 per seal or stamp, ask if the notary is aware of the New Mexico law that regulates fees. The law on notaries public is discussed in more detail on page 116.

successor agent. People who have no spouse or children should appoint someone they trust. Second marriages can pose problems if a person wants to name the new spouse, and the children from the first marriage do not trust the new spouse. Some people may wish to appoint an agent who is not an immediate family member. This situation may arise if (1) relationships between immediate family members are estranged, (2) couples in non-traditional relationships, such as those who live together without being married or homosexual couples, wish to appoint a longtime companion as their agent, (3) a person has no immediate family members, or (4) a person wishes to appoint a good, trusted friend as an agent even if the person has family members who could serve.

There is no requirement that you appoint the same person as your agent for health care powers and financial powers. Many individuals appoint one person to make health care decisions for them and a different person or bank to make financial decisions.

There is no requirement that you appoint an immediate family member as your agent. If you sign a power of attorney making an unusual designation of an agent, family members may object and could challenge the power of attorney in court. If the power of attorney is valid and the agent is acting properly, it is hoped the judge would honor your appointment of agent.

If you do not create a power of attorney appointing an agent, and you become incapacitated, state law will automatically appoint a health care decision-maker. This person may or may not have been your choice. If you have no financial power of attorney or other management plan in place, family members can go to court and seek to be appointed as your conservator, even if you would not want those family members appointed. (Guardians and conservators are discussed in detail beginning on page 22.)

One way to help avoid a challenge to the power of attorney is to sign it in the presence of two witnesses. New Mexico law does not require a power of attorney to be witnessed, but using witnesses may make the power of attorney harder to challenge. While people can always go to court to challenge a document, they do not always win. Also, instead of appointing an individual as your agent, you might appoint a bank, trust company or agency that acts as an agent for others. Appointing a neutral agent may help prevent challenges to a power of attorney.

Some questions to consider before appointing an agent include:

❑ Is the person familiar with my thoughts on health care, life support and other personal care decisions?

❑ Is the person familiar with my financial affairs?

❑ Do I have a good relationship with the person so that I can communicate my wishes and thoughts before I become incapacitated?

❑ Does the person have the skills and sophistication to handle my particular financial affairs? Does the person understand how to write checks, how to roll over a certificate of deposit, how to invest in the stock market, how to collect on a real estate contract?

❑ Is the person stable? Does the person have any problems, such as divorce, bankruptcy, alcohol or drug abuse, illness, emotional or mental health problems?

❑ Has the person treated me fairly and honestly in prior dealings?

❑ Does the person have the time to handle my affairs?

❑ Does the person live in the same town so that helping me would be relatively easy?

If the answer to several of these questions is no, you should reconsider your choice of agent.

Should My Agent Get Paid?

Some people ask if the agent is entitled to be paid for serving on behalf of the principal. Most power of attorney documents do not state whether the agent is to be paid. If you have strong feelings one way or the other, you should state them in the power of attorney document. Often agents are family members who do not expect to be paid. Banks or other corporate entities that serve as agents receive reasonable compensation.

One possible way to provide some oversight of your agent is to include an accounting provision in the financial power of attorney. You might require the agent to provide an accounting of financial transactions and bills paid on your behalf quarterly, semiannually or annually. The agent could provide this information to other family members, to an accountant or to a trusted friend. Some agents may view an accounting provision as burdensome or as a sign that you do not trust them. Others may understand that it is an attempt to protect yourself from mismanagement or to provide information and communication to people who were not chosen as your agent.

Responsibilities of Agent

Agents have a duty to act honestly and prudently. **Despite agents' personal views, agents should make decisions for principals that the principals would make for themselves, if they were able.** The agent is standing in the shoes of the principal and is to act on the principal's behalf. The agent cannot use the principal's money for the agent's personal needs, such as paying for a trip to Hawaii or buying the agent a car. The agent can only use the principal's money for the principal's care and family. The agent must make health care decisions for the principal that the principal would want. Even if the agent does not believe in using artificial life support equipment, if the principal wanted such equipment used, the agent should authorize it.

Despite these duties and responsibilities, some agents break the law and do not act in the best interest of the principal. An agent can be sued in court for converting the principal's assets for the agent's own use or for misusing the principal's assets. In reality, however, if the agent has misused assets and is unable to pay them back, the principal may be out of luck. In cases of extreme misuse of funds, the district attorney may prosecute the agent. But a criminal proceeding would not necessarily recover the assets.

Another way to stop an agent who is misusing a power of attorney is to go to court and ask the judge to appoint a conservator (see page 22) for the incapacitated principal. New Mexico law allows a fiduciary (conservator, trustee, etc.) to revoke or amend a power of attorney if the court expressly authorizes this after notice to the agent and incapacitated person. The conservator could *revoke* the power of attorney and end the agent's power if the court gave specific written permission to do so.

Powers of attorney can be dangerous instruments if they fall into the wrong hands. Manipulative or dishonest people can use a power of attorney to take away the principal's assets to benefit themselves rather than the principal. Appointing a **trustworthy** agent to make health care and financial decisions for you is **vital**. (See page 32 for information on possible liability for serving as an agent.)

Do-It-Yourself Power of Attorney (New Mexico Form)

The New Mexico Legislature passed a law that allows a do-it-yourself power of attorney. The Appendix to this book contains a sample copy of the do-it-yourself New Mexico power of attorney form (Appendix 2—Forms, Form 1). The form includes blanks for appointing a first-choice agent and a second-choice agent. This power of attorney form contains a list of powers that the principal can initial. Beside each of the powers is a ( ) where the principal can initial to authorize that particular power. The form also includes a paragraph about when the power of attorney becomes effective, a place for the principal to sign, a line for the date and a place for the notary public to sign. The form includes some instructions and is supposed to be self-explanatory, but here are a few things to consider:

❏ An **attorney-in-fact** is the person you appoint to act for you. Other power of attorney forms may call this person an **agent**.

❏ While you put your initials in the ( ) to designate which powers you want your attorney-in-fact to have, you might want to draw a line through the entire power and ( ) if you do **not** want the attorney-in-fact to have that power. This will prevent anyone from filling in this power later.

❑ The form includes "tax matters, including any transactions with the Internal Revenue Service" as a power to give to an agent. This language may not meet IRS guidelines. Tax matters are discussed in more detail on page 14.

❑ If this power of attorney will be used to sell real estate, you must RECORD it at the county clerk's office where the property is located. New Mexico law requires this recording so the public has notice that your attorney-in-fact has the power to sell your home.

❑ Just above the (Signature) line is a paragraph that you can sign if you want the power of attorney to be in effect ONLY if you become incapacitated. If you do not check and initial this paragraph, the power of attorney will be in effect from the moment you sign.

❑ As mentioned above, do not sign this power of attorney unless a notary is present. Do not pay more than $5.00 per acknowledgment to the notary. (*See also* footnote 4, page 3.)

❑ On the back of New Mexico's do-it-yourself power of attorney form is an "Affidavit As To Power of Attorney Being in Full Force" (see Appendix 2—Forms, Form 1). Your agent could fill in this section prior to using the power of attorney. In reality, businesses that rely on the power of attorney usually do not require the agent to fill out this section. On the other hand, a few businesses have required certification that the principal is still alive and that the power of attorney is still in effect.

One power on the do-it-yourself New Mexico power of attorney form allows the agent to transfer property to a spouse. Federal and state laws permit certain transfers of property between spouses and other people to become eligible for government benefits that pay for nursing home care. For proper planning you should consider having a similar provision in your power of attorney, especially if you are married. Be aware, however, that this provision may not be appropriate for all married couples. In second marriages one spouse may not wish to have all of his or her separate assets transferred to the healthy spouse, but would rather have the assets transferred to the children from the first marriage. Chapter Three discusses issues of spousal impoverishment and payment of nursing home care in great detail.

You are not required to use this do-it-yourself form in New Mexico. You may use a more detailed power of attorney for health care and/or financial matters. People who have substantial assets, such as stocks, bonds or real estate, may benefit from a more comprehensive power of attorney tailored to their needs and assets. Certain stockbrokers or banks may prefer that you use their own form.

Health Care Powers of Attorney

Older powers of attorney may not mention health care decisions. However, two powers included in the do-it-yourself New Mexico power of attorney form authorize an agent to make health care decisions for a principal. Then in 1995 the New Mexico legislature passed the Uniform Health-Care Decisions Act (UHCDA).[5] UHCDA also contains provisions for health care powers of attorney. Therefore, New Mexico has two different ways to create a health care power of attorney.

For **health care decisions**, New Mexicans may now: (1) use the do-it-yourself New Mexico power of attorney form, initial the health care powers (as well as whatever financial powers you wish to allow), and sign the form in the presence of a notary public; or (2) fill out a separate health care power of attorney that contains only health care powers.[6]

---

[5]Chapter Two discusses UHCDA in depth.

[6]As of July 1, 1995, competent individuals may also orally appoint a person (called a "surrogate") to make health care decisions on their behalf. A surrogate

Law Regarding Health Care Powers of Attorney

UHCDA only requires a health care power of attorney to be "in writing and signed by the principal." Although UHCDA does not require the health care power of attorney to be notarized or witnessed, having two witnesses sign is recommended. Having witnesses may prevent fraud or forgery, make the document harder to challenge and help it be honored in another state.

A competent individual may revoke this health care power of attorney either by a signed writing or by personally informing the health care provider. A sample optional form is included in the UHCDA, and a similar form is included in this book (Appendix 2—Forms, Form 3). Appendix 1—Resources contains information about where to order full-size copies of an optional form similar to the UHCDA form.

If you have already signed a durable health care power of attorney, right to die statement, and/or other advance health care directive, you do not need a new form.

The agent appointed by the principal should make health care decisions in accordance with the principal's instructions and other wishes, if known; otherwise, the agent should make health care decisions that are in the principal's best interest.

Health care providers may be caught in the middle if the agent seeks one treatment and other family members seek a different treatment. **Communication with family members and friends is essential.** Let them know you have signed a health care power. Give them guidance about how to make decisions for you. Ask that they follow **your** wishes, not their own, in making health care decisions for you. Also explore your doctor's opinions about discontinuing life support systems and other treatment. Make sure

---

may make health care decisions for an incapacitated patient who has not appointed an agent through a health care power of attorney or who does not have a court-appointed guardian. Chapter Two discusses surrogates in more detail.

that your doctor understands your wishes and philosophies, and will honor your wishes. If you and your doctor disagree on quality of life issues (for instance, your doctor may believe in trying all treatments no matter what your wishes), you should consider finding a doctor whose views are more compatible with your own.

Values History Form—Guiding Your Agent

The University of New Mexico's Health Sciences Center Ethics Program has developed a **Values History Form** to help you think about and write down your feelings about your health care. Filling out this form requires a lot of thought and prompts you to think about specific medical procedures, your attitude toward life, your personal relationships and other sensitive areas. But filling out the form will help guide whomever you choose as your agent. It may also generate helpful discussions between you and your family, as well as between you and your agent. The Appendix to this book contains a sample copy of the values history form (Appendix 2— Forms, Form 2) and information about where to obtain a full-size copy, if you prefer.

Federal Law Relating to Powers of Attorney

In 1990 Congress amended federal Medicare and Medicaid law by adding **The Patient Self-Determination Act**. Effective December 1, 1991, the Act requires all Medicare and Medicaid provider organizations (such as hospitals, skilled nursing facilities, home health agencies, hospices and prepaid health care organizations) to:

❑ Provide written information to patients at the time of admission concerning the right to make decisions about medical care, including the right to accept or refuse treatment and the right to make advance directives, such as powers of attorney and living wills.

❑ Maintain written policies and procedures about advance directives and to inform patients of the policies.

❑ Document in the patient's medical record whether or not the individual has executed an advance directive.

❑ Ensure compliance with state law regarding advance directives (this means the organization should recognize and comply with a valid living will or power of attorney).

❑ Provide education for staff and the community on issues concerning advance directives (this includes a provision that **New Mexico**, through an agency or other organization, develop a written description of state law on advance directives that Medicare and Medicaid providers would then distribute).

This act should help further public awareness and use of powers of attorney and other advance health care directives. The act does **not** require people to sign a health care power of attorney or other advance directive in order to be admitted to the hospital or nursing facility. The act merely requires facilities to **inform** patients about their rights and about what documents are available under state law.

Financial Powers of Attorney

A financial power of attorney can be very broad. If you only want your agent to handle certain financial matters, you should sign a **limited** power of attorney. Be aware that if you become incapacitated and your power of attorney is not broad enough for your agent to handle your affairs, your family may have to go to court to have a guardian or conservator appointed. Some powers of attorney include safeguards, such as prohibiting the agent from:

❑ Giving a stockbroker discretionary stock powers. This means your agent could not give a stockbroker unlimited power to conduct transactions without first getting permission from the agent.

❑ Changing an existing estate plan. Your agent could not change the beneficiaries of your will.

❑ Interfering with an existing trust. The trust would control assets that are part of the trust.

❑ Making gifts of the principal's property unless the gifts meet special guidelines that may also be specified in the power of attorney.

Some businesses are leery of relying on a power of attorney, especially when it is used to sell real estate or stock. Insurance matters and tax matters may also pose special problems. If you want your agent to be able to sell your home or land, you should **identify the home or land by its address or legal description.** This will make the title company more likely to honor the power of attorney. Not all title companies are willing to provide title insurance when real estate is sold by your agent, rather than you, but your agent should be able to find a title company that will honor the power of attorney.

Also, some stock companies prefer that their own power of attorney form be used. This might prove burdensome if you have stocks or bonds with several different brokerage firms. A conflict might also arise between your regular financial power of attorney and the power of attorney you fill out for the stockbroker, **especially if you have appointed different people to serve as your agent in each power of attorney**. If you must fill out a separate power of attorney for your stockbroker and you **intend** to choose an agent different than your health care or other financial agent, be sure you state this intention clearly in the power of attorney.

A brokerage firm may also be willing to honor your general financial power of attorney if it includes the power to sell stocks and bonds. Listing your holdings by name may help, but if you sell them, you do not want to have to update the power of attorney each time. So if your power of attorney lists specific stocks and bonds, it should also say, "including, but not limited to, the following stocks and bonds." Talk to your broker **before** you sign a power of attorney to see if the broker will honor it. If you have already signed a power of attorney, show a copy to your broker and ask if the broker will honor it if you become incapacitated.

Insurance companies also require a specific reference in the power of attorney to the authority of the agent to transfer ownership of the policy, cash in the policy, change a beneficiary or make any other disposition under the policy. Listing the name of the insurance company and policy number may help insure that the insurance company will honor the power of attorney.

People have had some problems with the Internal Revenue Service (IRS) when attempting to use a power of attorney to file and sign someone else's income tax return. The IRS will honor a valid power of attorney that includes the power to handle tax matters, including the type of tax involved (income tax, estate tax, etc.), the tax years covered, the tax form numbers included (such as Form 1040, Schedules A, B, C, etc.), and what tax matters the agent may handle (such as filing and signing the return). You should check your existing power of attorney to see if tax matters are listed as a power given to your agent.

If your power of attorney does not mention tax matters, you might consider filling out a special IRS power of attorney Form 2848. IRS Forms are available free by calling 1-800-829-3676. Even if your power of attorney does mention tax matters, the IRS may not allow an agent **other than a spouse** to sign tax returns unless you have filled out Form 2848 because the IRS is particular about the information required in the power of attorney. The IRS does allow spouses to sign each other's names without a power of attorney in the case of illness or injury. Contact the IRS, 1-800-829-1040, for more information.

Honoring the Power of Attorney

Currently no New Mexico law requires a bank, stockbroker or other organization to honor a power of attorney. However, if a power of attorney is valid, the agent could sue the company in court and attempt to force it to honor the power of attorney. This would be time consuming and expensive. Showing the power of attorney to your bank, stockbroker, insurance company or other company **before** your agent has to use the power of attorney may prevent problems later. Starting a conservatorship proceeding in court might be another option.

Some attorneys report that it has become difficult to rely on powers of attorney. Some New Mexico banks will not allow an agent to access a safety deposit box unless the power of attorney specifically says "safety deposit box." Some banks will not allow an agent to set up an income diversion trust account (used in nursing home planning) unless the power of attorney includes the power to "create an irrevocable trust."

Every state has a law regarding powers of attorney, but many states have different requirements. Some states' laws contain power of attorney forms. Others require witnesses or disclosure statements (warnings about how dangerous a power of attorney can be). Some states, such as California, require the legal description of a house or land to be included in the power of attorney in order for the agent to use the power of attorney to sell that property.

If you move to another state will your New Mexico power of attorney be honored? In most cases the answer is probably "yes." Some states have specific laws that say out-of-state powers of attorney will be honored. But if you lived in New Mexico, owned land in California and had a power of attorney signed in New Mexico that did not include the legal description of your land in California, then California would probably not allow your agent to sell the land. Other variations in state law might cause similar problems if you relocate.[7]

To be safe, if you move to another state sign a new power of attorney that meets the requirements of the new state's law. If you move to another state and are no longer competent to make a new power of attorney, your agent will have to use the old power of attorney. If a business does not honor the old power of attorney,

---

[7]Trusts, discussed in detail in Chapter Five, can help avoid potential problems when people own property in several states or move from state to state.

your agent or family might have to start a conservatorship proceeding in the new state.

If you made a power of attorney in another state, will New Mexico honor it? The legislature passed a law that says if an out of state power of attorney was valid in the state where it was created, it will be deemed valid here if it is "not inconsistent with the public policy of this state."

Recording Power of Attorney

Normally, powers of attorney do **not** need to be recorded. If, however, the agent will use the power of attorney to handle any real estate transactions, New Mexico law requires that the power of attorney be **recorded** in the Office of the County Clerk where the land is located. Each county in New Mexico has a county clerk whose employees handle the recording and filing of various documents. The current charge for recording one page (regular size or legal size paper) is $9.00. Each additional page costs $2.00 to record. The purpose of recording documents is to establish a public record giving **notice** to everyone about the recorded document. For example, deeds to property must be recorded into the county record so that title can be traced for every piece of property. Recording a power of attorney would give the public notice that your agent has authority to sign any real property papers and conduct other business on your behalf.

Separate Documents

Although New Mexico's do-it-yourself power of attorney form combines health care and financial powers onto one form, many people prefer to do separate forms. Some people sign detailed health care powers of attorney and financial powers of attorney specially tailored to the assets of the estate. A financial power of attorney may include account numbers, stock holdings and real estate descriptions, which the principals do not want the hospital or doctor to know. The hospital or doctor only needs to know about health care powers. Several banks and trust companies have stated that they prefer separate documents because the health care provisions are irrelevant to the financial powers.

Also, if you have appointed **different** agents for health care and financial powers, it makes sense to sign separate documents. If you have powers of attorney that become effective at different times (i.e., your health care power of attorney goes into effect **only if** you become incapacitated, but the financial power of attorney is currently in effect), you may want separate documents. Combining the two sets of powers into one document is certainly legal but may prove inconvenient for the people or businesses relying on the power of attorney for different purposes.

Special Power of Attorney Regarding a Minor Child

New Mexico law provides three ways to appoint a guardian for an unmarried minor. A parent may sign a power of attorney and delegate to another person any of the parent's powers regarding the care, custody or property of the minor child. The parents **cannot** delegate their power to consent to the marriage or adoption of the minor child. Under state law this power of attorney can remain in effect for six months, after which time the parent would have to sign an updated power of attorney. A power of attorney might be useful if: (1) the parents of a child were out of the country temporarily; (2) the parent faced surgery or other circumstance that might render the parent temporarily incapacitated; or (3) the child were living outside of the home with another family.

Parents can also name a guardian for a minor child in their will or in another writing signed by the parent and attested by at least two witnesses. The child, under state law, has some power to object to the appointment. Finally, the court may also appoint a guardian for an unmarried minor "if all parental rights of custody have been terminated or suspended by circumstances or prior court order." This third method is outside the scope of this book.

Scope of Power of Attorney

A power of attorney may be **limited** or it may be very **general**. A limited power of attorney might authorize a single transaction, such as the sale of a house or the transfer of a bond. A limited power of attorney might allow someone to pay your bills while you are on an extended trip. Or the power of attorney might cover any and all business, money, health care and personal matters. A broad power of attorney is considered a general power of attorney. You should carefully analyze your needs and situation to determine what power of attorney will best help you. A skilled attorney can often save you and your family headaches and money by advising you and preparing suitable documents for you.

Effective Date of Power of Attorney

A power of attorney can either be in effect **immediately** from the moment you sign it or can **spring** into effect **only if** you become incapacitated. A power of attorney that goes into effect only if you need it is called a **springing power of attorney**.

Regarding *financial* decisions, you might want a power of attorney in effect immediately if you are immobile or out of town and need your agent to handle money matters for you. Otherwise, many people wish to manage their own financial affairs while they are able and to rely on an agent only if they become incapacitated.

Regarding *health care* decisions, most people want to make their own health care decisions as long as they are able. If you want an agent to handle money matters for you now but you want to continue to make your own health care decisions, you may want to sign **separate** health care and financial powers of attorney.

Before you sign a power of attorney, you should decide whether you want the power of attorney to take effect immediately or to take effect only upon your future disability or incapacity. If the power of attorney takes effect **only if** you become incapacitated, the document should define incapacity and state who determines whether you are incapacitated. For example, New Mexico's do-it-yourself power of attorney form says that your agent must obtain notarized statements from two qualified health care professionals regarding your incapacity. This requirement may seem burdensome, but it is intended to protect you. If you do not say when the power of attorney goes into effect, the power of attorney is effective immediately.

What Does Durable Mean?

Durable means that the power of attorney stays in effect *even if the principal becomes incapacitated.* To be durable, the power of attorney **must** include a sentence stating that the power of attorney "shall not be affected by subsequent incapacity of the principal, or lapse of time" or a sentence stating that the power of attorney "shall become effective upon the incapacity of the principal" or similar words. Including one of these sentences (or similar words) means the power of attorney remains **durable** if you are incapacitated in the future. New Mexico law states that unless a power of attorney contains a time of termination, it remains in effect no matter how much time has lapsed since signing it.

If the durability clause is omitted from the power of attorney, the agent will no longer be authorized to act for you if you become incapacitated. Some powers of attorney signed years ago do not include this clause about durability and should be updated. It would be unfortunate if a power of attorney ended when you became incapacitated—the very time you most need help with financial and health care matters.

Costs of Powers of Attorney

The costs of powers of attorney vary greatly. Some attorneys charge per document. Charges range from $50 to $100 and up per document, depending on how detailed the document is. Other attorneys include the cost of a power of attorney in a package that includes a will or trust, powers of attorney and health care directives.

Signing a power of attorney yourself is inexpensive, especially if you obtain the forms at little or no cost. The cost of the do-it-yourself New Mexico form is about a $1.50 per copy. Appendix 1—Resources contains information about where to order a health care power of attorney form for little or no cost.

If your estate is large or you have unusual circumstances, consider hiring an attorney to assess your needs and draft the appropriate document. **If someone is trying to force you to appoint him or her as your agent, see an attorney to protect your rights.** If you sign a **financial** power of attorney without an attorney's help, make sure you sign in the presence of a notary public, who notarizes the power of attorney. Otherwise, the power of attorney will not be valid.

Revoking Power of Attorney

People who have created a power of attorney may **revoke** that power of attorney at any time, as long as they are competent to understand what they are doing. People who revoke their **financial** power of attorney should put the revocation **in writing** and sign the revocation **in the presence of a notary public.** The revocation should then be sent to any bank, stockbroker or other person or business relying on the power of attorney so that they have **notice** that they should not rely on the power of attorney anymore. The written revocation must also be **recorded** in the Office of the County Clerk if the original power of attorney was recorded.

Powers of attorney end at the principal's death. But New Mexico law provides that if a bank (or other entity relying on the power of attorney) does not **receive notice** of the principal's death or disability, it cannot be liable for acting in good faith under the power of attorney. This New Mexico law protects the bank or other entity if it acts on the power of attorney without **knowing** that it was revoked. After the bank or other entity knows that the principal has died, it can no longer honor the power of attorney. The personal representative designated in the principal's will or trust would then take over the principal's affairs.

Other Ways to Manage Property

Trusts. Trusts, discussed in more detail in Chapter Five, may provide management of a person's financial affairs during both times of health and illness. Some trusts name a relative, accountant, friend or other person to serve as trustee and manage the financial affairs, or a person may name a bank, trust company or other corporate entity to manage the estate. Corporate trustees charge a management fee based on the size of the trust and may not wish to manage small (less than $100,000) estates.

Bank Accounts. Many single people add one child's name to their bank accounts as a joint tenant. If the person dies, the remaining joint tenant automatically receives the proceeds in the account. The person may want the additional name on the account so that the child can pay the bills but may intend for the proceeds of the account to be divided among all of the children. (Chapter Four discusses some hazards of joint tenancy.) A little known New Mexico law allows a person to set up a **bank account** that allows another person to pay the bills but not to receive the proceeds of the account. The proceeds of the account would pass according to the terms of the person's will. People who set up this arrangement with the bank must do so in writing and must make their intent very clear. The bank keeps the instructions with the person's signature card at the bank. A copy of the instructions should also be kept with the person's will. Keep in mind that adding another person to a bank account only allows that person to access that particular account. To file income taxes, sell stocks or perform other financial matters, the person would have to give another person a financial power of attorney.

Representative Payee. A representative payee is someone you name to receive a benefits check on your behalf. The Social Security Administration and the Veteran's Administration allow the appointment of a representative payee to receive and spend benefits on behalf of someone who is incapacitated. The representative payee is now required to file an annual accounting of all money received and spent. Appointing a representative payee who is honest and concerned about the incapacitated person is one way to avoid more restrictive types of management. However, the representative payee will only be able to handle the Social Security or Veteran's Administration benefits and not other financial or health matters. Representative payees who have a power of attorney for the incapacitated person can also handle other financial and health matters.

Guardianship or Conservatorship

A guardianship and/or conservatorship proceeding[8] is a court proceeding during which a person seeks to have a guardian appointed to make health care decisions and/or a conservator appointed to make financial decisions for an incapacitated person. Because of the seriousness of the procedure and the court involvement, guardianships and conservatorships are probably the most restrictive management method for incapacitated people. People who have never been in a courtroom before may experience additional stress and anxiety.

Compared to powers of attorney, guardianship and conservatorship proceedings are expensive and time consuming. On the other hand, a power of attorney does not take away the power of the principal to conduct business. The principal could still write checks, make investments and conduct other financial transactions even if the agent were also acting for the principal. When the principal acts inappropriately, such as giving away assets or mismanaging funds, a conservatorship may be necessary. If the court imposes a full conservatorship on the principal, the principal

---

[8]New Mexico's law on guardianships and conservatorships appears in the New Mexico Statutes Annotated, Sections 45-5-101 through 45-5-433. These statutes are available at the University of New Mexico School of Law Library (Albuquerque), the New Mexico Supreme Court Library (Santa Fe), the New Mexico State University Library located in Branson Hall (Las Cruces) and at various attorneys' offices. You may also purchase copies of these statutes directly from the New Mexico Compilation Commission, PO Box 15549, Santa Fe NM 87506; (505) 827-4821.

will no longer be able to handle financial matters. The conservatorship offers more protection for an incapacitated person, but it also takes away more rights of the person.

A guardianship or conservatorship may also be appropriate if an incapacitated person is being abused, neglected or exploited by family members or others. New Mexico has laws prohibiting the abuse, neglect and exploitation of others, but a discussion of these laws is outside the scope of this book. Those who suspect a vulnerable person is being exploited, abused or neglected should contact their local Human Services Department, Adult Protective Services Division, for information. If you cannot find the local number, contact the state Human Services Department, 1-800-432-6217.

The American Bar Association commissioned a national study on guardianships and conservatorships. The study revealed that in many instances courts had imposed guardianships and/or conservatorships on individuals who were not incapacitated. Also, incapacitated people sometimes did not receive notice of the proceeding and did not have an opportunity to present their side to the court. As a result of this study, many states examined their laws on guardianships and conservatorships and revised the laws to better protect individuals.

The New Mexico legislature revised its guardianship and conservatorship laws in an effort to provide more protection for the alleged incapacitated person. Some people feel that these revisions protect the civil rights of the alleged incapacitated person; others feel the requirements are too expensive and unnecessary. Current New Mexico law allows the court to impose a guardianship or con-servatorship on a person only if it is the least restrictive alternative.

The law also allows the court to impose a **limited guardianship and/or conservatorship** tailored to the specific needs of the individual. A person for whom a limited guardian or conservator is appointed retains all legal and civil rights except those specifically granted to the limited guardian or conservator by the court.

What are Guardians and Conservators?

The court may appoint a **guardian** to make *personal and health care decisions* for a person who is so impaired for reasons such as mental illness, physical disability or alcohol abuse that the person cannot make personal care decisions.[9] New Mexico law states that a guardianship should encourage the individual's independence and should be limited to the powers necessary to accommodate the person's actual functional mental and physical limitations. A **conservator** is a person appointed by the court to manage the *property or financial affairs* of an incapacitated person or minor ward.[10]

Who Should Serve as Guardian/Conservator?

Often a spouse will serve as guardian or conservator for an incapacitated spouse. If no spouse is alive or willing to serve, a child who is over the age of eighteen may serve. If the incapacitated person is single, has no children or has children who are unfamiliar with the incapacitated person's affairs, a friend, accountant, banker or other person may be an appropriate choice to serve as conservator. Usually bankers or accountants will **not** serve as a guardian because they do not feel qualified to make health care or personal care decisions for customers. Not all children have the best interests of their parents at heart. A child who has substance abuse problems such as alcohol or drug addiction or who is going through divorce or bankruptcy proceedings may not be the best choice to serve as guardian or conservator.

New Mexico law does not require that the guardian and conservator be the same person or corporation. One person may

---

[9]The New Mexico Uniform Health-Care Decisions Act should reduce the need for guardianships, but not conservatorships. The Act is discussed briefly in this Chapter and in more detail in Chapter Two.

[10]New Mexico law defines a ward as a person for whom a guardian has been appointed.

serve as the guardian and another as the conservator. A bank may serve as conservator, while an adult child serves as guardian. In many cases, the guardian and conservator will be the same person. Those who serve as guardian and/or conservator should be trusted individuals who have knowledge of the incapacitated person's feelings about health care as well as the skills and sophistication to handle the incapacitated person's financial affairs. If the incapacitated person's estate is over $100,000, a bank or trust company may be a wise choice to serve as conservator. Because banks and trust companies usually will not agree to make *health care decisions*, a family member or friend would handle the personal care decisions and the bank or trust company would handle financial decisions.

The Guardianship/Conservatorship Court Proceeding

Certain court papers called **pleadings** must be filed in every guardianship or conservatorship case. If the person needs both a guardian and conservator, the two proceedings are often combined into one. Any person interested in the estate, affairs or welfare of the person to be protected can start a guardianship and/or conservatorship proceeding by contacting an attorney familiar with this area of the law. The person who starts the proceeding is called the **petitioner**.

A typical guardianship and conservatorship proceeding will involve the following steps:

❏ **Petition for Appointment of a Guardian and Conservator**: This document provides detailed information about the petitioner, the person to be protected, information on the person's assets, the proposed guardian and conservator, and the closest relatives of the person who may need protection. The petition is filed in the district court in the county where the alleged incapacitated person resides. The court will assign the case to a judge and give the petition a case number that will appear on all future papers filed in the court.

❑ **Order for Hearing and Appointments**: This order, signed by the judge, will state the time, date and place of the hearing on the guardianship and conservatorship proceeding, and the names of the *guardian ad litem*, visitor and qualified health care professional to be appointed. *Guardian ad litem*, visitor and qualified health care professional are defined below.

❑ **Notice of Hearing**: A copy of the Notice of Hearing and a copy of the Petition for Appointment and the Order for Hearing must be **personally** served (handed to the person and a sworn proof of service filed with the court) on the alleged incapacitated person, **even if the person is incapable of understanding the document**. The alleged incapacitated person's spouse and parents (if they can be found within New Mexico) are also entitled to **personal service** of these documents. The notice must be served at least **fourteen days** before the date of hearing. If the spouse and parents are not in New Mexico, notice must be mailed to them or published in a newspaper's legal notices section. Adult children, at least one close relative, and a previously appointed guardian or conservator, custodian or caretaker must also receive notice by mail or publication in a newspaper. If the alleged incapacitated person lives in a nursing home or shelter care home, then the administrator of the home must also be served with notice.

❑ *Guardian ad litem*: The court will appoint a **guardian ad litem** for the alleged incapacitated person. The *guardian ad litem* must be an attorney. The duties of the *guardian ad litem* include representing the alleged incapacitated person and presenting that person's views to the court, as well as making recommendations that best protect the interests of the alleged incapacitated person. The *guardian ad litem* must also (1) interview in person the alleged incapacitated person; (2) interview the qualified health care professional, visitor and proposed guardian; (3) review the written reports submitted by the qualified health care professional and visitor; and (4) obtain independent medical or psychological assessments, or both, if necessary.

The *guardian ad litem* may decide that a guardianship/conservatorship is unnecessary or that the proposed guardian/conservator is not a wise choice. The *guardian ad litem* usually spends five to ten hours on a case, depending on the difficulty of the case.

New Mexico law states that the *guardian ad litem* is entitled to be paid from the alleged incapacitated person's assets. If that person has no assets, some attorneys do a limited number of *pro bono* cases (at no charge). Sometimes family members will chip in and pay the *guardian ad litem*, as well as the attorney who files the papers. Usually, the attorney for the petitioner will recommend to the court the name of an attorney who has already agreed to serve as *guardian ad litem*. The *guardian ad litem* may also be an attorney who has served the alleged incapacitated person in the past. The *guardian ad litem* must sign a Consent to Serve before a notary public and file the consent with the court.

❑ **Court Visitor**: The court will also appoint a **visitor** to interview the alleged incapacitated person and submit a written report to the court. The visitor (usually a nurse, social worker or someone familiar with various incapacities of people) must interview the alleged incapacitated person, interview the person seeking appointment as guardian and must also visit the present residence of the alleged incapacitated person and the proposed residence if a change in residence is being considered. The visitor may also advise the court whether appointing a guardian or conservator is appropriate. The visitor will assess the person's ability to make personal care decisions, such as dressing, bathing, eating and taking medicines. The visitor may also assess the person's ability to handle finances, balance a checkbook and pay bills.

Current fees for a court visitor range from $50 to $100 per hour. The visitor usually spends four to ten hours to complete all interviews and reports. Sometimes a social worker at a nursing home where the alleged incapacitated person resides, a social worker with Adult Protective Services (a division of the New

Mexico Human Services Department) or the case manager of an outreach program that is helping the person serves as a court visitor for free. Having a visitor who knows the alleged incapacitated person can be helpful.

❑ **Qualified Health Care Professional**: The court will appoint a **qualified health care professional** to examine the alleged incapacitated person. The qualified health care professional may be a physician or nurse practitioner. The health care professional must submit to the court a written evaluation that must contain certain information required by New Mexico law. This information includes a detailed report about the alleged incapacitated person's incapacity and what tasks the person is capable of doing with or without assistance. Most physicians who have cared for the alleged incapacitated person for a while will not charge to complete the required report. Others may charge $50 or more.

❑ **Hearing and Order**: The judge will hold a hearing on the petition and will accept evidence such as the written reports of the qualified health care professional and the visitor, the written or oral report from the *guardian ad litem*, and other evidence provided by anyone involved in the proceeding. If the proceeding is **uncontested** (everyone agrees the guardianship or conservatorship is necessary and that the proposed guardian and conservator is appropriate), usually the qualified health care professional will not attend the hearing. The visitor usually attends the hearing and may make an oral as well as written report to the judge. The general public is not allowed to attend a guardianship or conservatorship proceeding in order to protect the privacy of the alleged incapacitated person.

After a full hearing, if the judge finds that the person is incapacitated, that no less restrictive alternatives are available and that the appointment of a guardian and conservator is appropriate, the judge can appoint a **full or limited guardian and conservator**. A full guardian or conservator would have all of the powers allowed under New Mexico law. A limited guardian would have some, but not all, of the powers allowed under New Mexico law. A limited conservator would have some, but not all, of the powers allowed under New Mexico law. The judge would tailor the order by defining the limitations on the guardian or conservator. The incapacitated person under a limited guardianship or conservatorship would be allowed to retain some control over his or her affairs. The judge would tailor the order by defining the limitations on the guardian and conservator. *If the guardian is to have complete authority over the incapacitated person's health care matters, all court orders made after July 1, 1995 should state that the guardian's powers override any powers given to an agent previously appointed under a power of attorney.*

❑ **Letters of Guardianship and Conservatorship**: The newly appointed guardian and conservator must sign an **Acceptance of Appointment**, which is filed with the court. The court clerk will then issue a paper called the **Letters of Guardianship and Conservatorship**. This document is official proof of the authority of the guardian and conservator to act for the incapacitated person. If the incapacitated person lives in a nursing home, the guardian should give a copy of the Letters to the nursing home administrator and to any doctor who has a medical file on the incapacitated person. The nursing home and doctor need to know whom to contact when a medical decision must be made for the incapacitated person. In a conservatorship case, banks and other financial institutions that work with the conservator will probably keep a copy of the Letters in their files.

Summary of Costs of Proceeding

Guardianship and conservatorship proceedings are expensive. The attorney for the petitioner usually charges by the hour. A routine, uncontested guardianship and/or conservatorship proceeding should take the attorney about ten hours. Some attorneys will charge a flat fee, no matter how many hours the attorney spends on the case. Fees must also be paid to the *guardian ad litem*, visitor (usually) and qualified health care professional (sometimes). In addition to these fees, there is a $122 fee ($107 in some judicial districts outside of Albuquerque) to file the case in court, and service of process fees from $25 to $50 per person served. New Mexico law states that the fees for the visitor, attorney, physician and conservator appointed in the proceeding are "entitled to reasonable compensation from the estate." **For an incapacitated individual with limited resources, paying all of these fees may be impossible. That is why it is best to have a power of attorney that covers health care and financial matters. If the power of attorney is valid, a guardianship and/or conservatorship proceeding is usually unnecessary.**

Duties of Guardian and Conservator

Before agreeing to serve, the proposed guardian and conservator should understand fully the duties involved. After someone is appointed as guardian and conservator for another, asking the attorney for a copy of New Mexico's laws that list the powers and duties may be wise. These duties include:

❑ Making all health care decisions for the incapacitated person, including surgery, treatment, medication, living arrangements, hiring doctors and nurses and whether or not to start or continue life support.

❑ Making all financial decisions for the incapacitated person. These duties vary depending on what kind of assets the person owns and might include paying bills, selling real estate, running a business, rolling over certificates of deposit or managing investment accounts, preparing and filing income tax returns, filing insurance claims and suing on behalf of the incapacitated person.

New Mexico law requires the guardian and conservator to file with the court:

❑ A complete inventory of the incapacitated person's estate within ninety days of appointment as conservator;

❑ An annual guardian and conservator's report; and

❑ An annual accounting of income, expenses and financial matters handled by the conservator.[11]

Emergency or Temporary Guardianship and/or Conservatorship

Sometimes if an alleged incapacitated person needs immediate medical attention or will suffer immediate physical or financial harm, an emergency guardianship and/or conservatorship proceeding may be appropriate. New Mexico law states basically that if waiting for a regular guardianship/conservatorship proceeding "would cause immediate and irreparable harm to the alleged incapacitated person's physical health [or to property or financial interests], the court may appoint a temporary guardian [or conservator] prior to the final hearing and decision on the petition." A concerned person (called the **petitioner**) will file a petition requesting appointment of a **temporary** guardian and/or conservator. The attorney and court will follow a procedure similar to the one outlined above, except that notice of the court hearing is not always given right away.

If no notice is given, the petition must include sworn statements (in writing or through testimony in court) from witnesses that support the petitioner's claim of irreparable harm. If the judge rules that the evidence presented shows irreparable harm would occur without the immediate appointment of a guardian or conservator, the judge will issue an order imposing a temporary guardianship or conservatorship upon the alleged incapacitated person. The alleged incapacitated person must then be notified **within 24 hours** of the appointment and has the right to contest it. A temporary guardianship or conservatorship usually cannot exceed sixty days unless the court orders an extension.

---

[11]A Guardianship and Conservatorship Manual, which outlines in detail the duties and responsibilities of those who serve, is available from the New Mexico Office of Guardianship, 1-800-311-2229.

Removal of Guardian/Conservator

The incapacitated person or any person interested in the person's welfare may petition the court for an order that the person is no longer incapacitated. The petition can seek the removal or resignation of the guardian and conservator. A proceeding may be appropriate if the incapacitated person gets better or if a guardian or conservator is making decisions that are not in the best interest of an incapacitated person. A person may request this order either by a formal petition or by an informal letter to the court. The court must appoint a visitor and qualified health care professional and should appoint a *guardian ad litem* to examine the incapacitated person and report to the court at the hearing to terminate the guardianship and/or conservatorship.

Liability of Agents and Guardians/Conservators

Those who serve as an agent through a power of attorney or as a guardian or conservator sometimes ask about their liability for serving. For example, if the agent signs papers to admit the principal to the hospital or nursing home, will the agent be personally liable for the principal's bills? Can the hospital or nursing home take the agent's own personal assets to pay the principal's bills?

Adult children are not generally responsible for the debts of their parents unless they have co-signed a loan or otherwise agreed to serve as guarantor of a loan for the parents. Similarly, parents are not responsible for the debts of their adult children. A person who serves as an agent for another is not responsible for the other person's debts **as long as it is clear from the papers the agent signs** that the agent is acting on behalf of the other person.

If you sign **"Principal's Name by Your Name, Agent"** or **"Your Name, as agent for Principal's Name,"** you should not be held personally liable. **Do not sign just your own name on a financial responsibility form for another!** In these instances, some hospitals have tried to make the signer personally liable for the other person's debts.

You might also consider crossing out any section that says "I am assuming financial responsibility for these bills." You might add at the bottom of the form **"I am not assuming personal financial responsibility for 'Principal's Name's' medical bills. Signed: Your Name."** *Be sure you read everything before you sign it.* As long as it is clear from the papers that you are signing as the agent (or guardian or conservator) on behalf of the principal, you should be protected from financial liability for the principal's debts.

New Mexico law outlines the powers and duties of guardians and conservators. A guardian is **not** legally obligated to provide his or her own funds for the incapacitated person and is not liable to third parties for the acts of the incapacitated person solely by reason of the guardianship. Those who serve should sign papers "as guardian and/or conservator for _____" to best protect themselves. Clearly stating one's authority may prevent future problems.

The idea of a guardianship and conservatorship frightens many people. Imposing a guardianship and conservatorship on someone results in the serious loss of a person's rights and control. No one should initiate a guardianship or conservatorship proceeding unless three things are true: (1) no other way to help the person exists, i.e., no power of attorney or other arrangements; (2) the person is seriously incapacitated and needs help; and (3) the person who seeks the appointment has the best interests of the incapacitated person, not his or her own interests, at heart.

Many families get along well and sincerely consider the best interests of their incapacitated family member. They make sure that a guardianship or conservatorship is necessary before starting the court proceeding. But not all family members get along. One person may try to use a guardianship or conservatorship proceeding to air family differences or to seek control of a person's finances. Using the time and resources of the court to conduct a family fight is a misuse of the judicial system. The costs of a **contested** guardianship and conservatorship can total thousands of dollars. The incapacitated person ends up being the loser, no matter what happens. Family relationships may become irreparably harmed. Sitting down and discussing frankly what is best for the incapacitated person and attempting to resolve issues before going to court is a wise idea. Going to court to get a guardian or conservator appointed can be intimidating and expensive. Before you go to court make sure that you are going for the right reasons.

2

HEALTH CARE DECISIONS IN NEW MEXICO

Adults have the right to make their own health care decisions, including seeking and refusing treatment. The U.S. Supreme Court has stated that a competent person, who understands the consequences, has the right to refuse medical treatment. Problems arise when an *incompetent* person has not expressed any wishes about life support or has not signed a power of attorney appointing an agent to make health care decisions. Who has the authority to make health care decisions for the incompetent person? How will the doctor know whether to insert a feeding tube? Should the doctor provide water, antibiotics, oxygen, a kidney machine or respirator as a means of prolonging the patient's life? What if the patient has been in a coma for years and without life support would die?

Uniform Health-Care Decisions Act

In 1995 the New Mexico legislature passed the Uniform Health-Care Decisions Act[1] ((UHCDA), which covers how most health care decisions are made in our state. UHCDA is meant to

---

[1]The Uniform Health-Care Decisions Act appears in the New Mexico Statutes Annotated, Sections 24-7A-1 through 24-7A-18. These statutes are available at the University of New Mexico School of Law Library (Albuquerque), the New Mexico Supreme Court Library (Santa Fe), the New Mexico State University Library located in Branson Hall (Las Cruces) and at various attorneys' offices. You may also purchase copies of these statutes directly from the New Mexico Compilation Commission, PO Box 15549, Santa Fe NM 87506; (505) 827-4821.

encourage health care providers to honor patients' wishes and should reduce the need for court-appointed guardianships.

Expressing Wishes About Health Care

One of the first statements in the law is that an adult who has capacity "has the right to make his or her own health-care decisions." Capacity is discussed on page 43. UHCDA allows individuals to give oral or written instructions about health care. A person must give oral instructions about health care treatment directly to a health care provider.

Although New Mexico law allows you to give oral instructions about your health care to your health care provider, it is much safer to make written instructions. Written instructions will help guide your decision-makers and doctors. Written instructions will also be harder to dispute when the time comes for others to make difficult decisions on your behalf.

Under UHCDA, **"health care decision"** means a decision made by an individual or the individual's agent, guardian or surrogate, regarding the individual's health care, including:

(1) selection and discharge of health care providers and institutions;

(2) approval or disapproval of diagnostic tests, surgical procedures, programs of medication and orders not to resuscitate;

(3) directions relating to life-sustaining treatment, including withholding or withdrawing life-sustaining treatment and the termination of life support; and

(4) directions to provide, withhold or withdraw artificial nutrition and hydration and all other forms of health care.

A person can give written instructions by signing: (1) a durable power of attorney for health care; (2) an optional form under UHCDA; or (3) any other form that complies with UHCDA. The optional form combines a health care power of attorney with individual instructions about health care, including end-of-life decisions. A sample optional form, similar to the UHCDA optional form, is included in this book (Appendix 2—Forms, Form 3). To avoid problems and conflicts, make sure you do not fill out several forms appointing different people to be your decision-maker.

Give copies of any written health care documents you make to your spouse, children or other close relatives or friends and to your doctor for your medical file. A copy should be available if you need to be admitted to the hospital.

Choosing a Health Care Decision-Maker

You can appoint a health care decision-maker three ways: (1) in writing, by appointing an **agent** under a power of attorney for health care; (2) by orally appointing a **surrogate**; or (3) by doing nothing, in which case UHCDA automatically appoints a surrogate for you.

Agent: An agent (sometimes called an "attorney-in-fact") is a person appointed in writing in a power of attorney to make decisions on your behalf. Chapter One discusses agents and powers of attorney in detail.

Surrogate: You can, if you have capacity, **orally** appoint a surrogate health care decision-maker by personally informing your primary doctor.[2] Unlike agents appointed in a power of attorney, appointing a surrogate does **not** require a writing.

Because of the oral appointment provisions, you do not have to sign any power of attorney form. Those who have strong feelings about who should make health care decisions on their behalf are probably wise to put their wishes in writing.

Automatic Surrogate: If: (1) you are incapacitated and do not have a written power of attorney; (2) you are incapacitated and have not orally named a surrogate decision-maker; or (3) the named agent, guardian or surrogate is unavailable,[3] UHCDA sets

---

[2]UHCDA's surrogate provisions appear to apply only if you are a patient in a health care facility and under a doctor's care. The law is silent about those who choose alternatives to traditional medicine.

[3]Some providers wonder how much effort they must make to locate an agent or surrogate. UHCDA says that agents or surrogates must be "reasonably

out who has priority to serve. Any member of the following classes of your family and friends, who is reasonably available, in descending order of priority, may act as your surrogate health care decision-maker: (1st) spouse, (2nd) significant other,[4] (3rd) an adult child, (4th) a parent, (5th) an adult brother or sister, (6th) a grandparent, (7th) an adult friend who knows your wishes.

Any surrogate must communicate his or her decision-making authority to the patient, patient's family and primary physician.

If there is a dispute or conflict among members of a class of surrogates, then a decision of a majority of the members of that class prevails. If the class is evenly divided in a dispute, then all members (**and** all individuals having lower priority) are disqualified from serving as surrogates,[5] and a guardianship proceeding, discussed in Chapter One, may be necessary.

One possible danger of this automatic process (which only applies if you have **not** appointed someone in writing or orally) is that the automatic surrogate might be someone you would not choose or who might not know your preferences. UHCDA does allow a patient **at any time** (capacitated or not) to disqualify

---

available" in order to act on behalf of a patient. This means the decision-maker is readily able to be contacted without undue effort and willing and able to act in a timely manner considering the urgency of the patient's health care needs. If an agent appointed in a health care power of attorney is not "reasonably available," then the automatic surrogate provisions of UHCDA would apply.

[4]UHCDA defines a significant other as "an individual in a long-term relationship of indefinite duration with the patient in which the individual has demonstrated an actual commitment to the patient similar to the commitment of a spouse and in which the individual and the patient consider themselves to be responsible for each other's well-being." The law allows doctors to ask for written proof of a relationship. This "significant other" provision applies to couples of all sexual orientations.

[5]For example, you have no spouse or significant other, but have four adult children. They are the class of surrogates with highest priority to serve. If two children want one treatment for you and two want a different treatment and they cannot agree, then all four children will be disqualified from serving as your surrogate, as will anyone else with a lower priority.

anyone from serving as a surrogate either by: (1) a signed writing; or (2) personally informing a health care provider.

How to Make Decisions for Another

Whether you are an agent or a surrogate, your job is to stand in the ill person's shoes and make health care decisions on behalf of that person. You should make health care decisions in accordance with the person's instructions and other wishes, if known. Check for written documents, ask family members to recall conversations about the person's wishes, try to apply that person's outlook and beliefs. Look for a Values History form, discussed on page 11, to guide you. Keep your own desires out of the decision-making process.

If you do not know the ill person's wishes, you should make health care decisions in that person's best interest, taking into account his or her personal values. While no set test exists for deciding the best interests of a person, consider whether a person has: a reversible condition; the ability to be rehabilitated; the ability to make human contact; any quality of life, no matter how minimal; pain; a disease the treatment of which would make the person suffer more. Medical, ethical, economic and religious issues, as well as legal issues, arise in cases involving the patient's best interest.

Some people have never been able to state their wishes; these cases are the most difficult. For people who have never had capacity, decision-makers must be especially careful when determining best interests. Withholding treatment **solely** because someone is old or disabled is inappropriate and discriminatory.

If you are an agent or surrogate for someone who is able to communicate, be sure and talk to him or her ahead of time. Before you agree to serve, make sure you are willing to follow that person's instructions, no matter what your personal beliefs are. Sometimes being an advocate for a patient is difficult, especially when other family members object to the decisions you are making. Talking about difficult topics with family members and decision-makers should help guide everyone toward following the patient's wishes.

Must the Doctor Follow My Wishes?

UHCDA states that doctors and other health care providers "shall comply" with your health care instructions, with limited exceptions. The doctor must follow instructions given by you (orally or in writing),[6] your agent, surrogate or guardian. UHCDA also imposes several record-keeping duties.

Doctors should write into your medical record whether you have:

- ❑ Any advance health care directives, including oral or written instructions and health care powers of attorney.
- ❑ Revoked any advance health care directives, either orally or in writing.
- ❑ Challenged a determination that you lack capacity (discussed below) or have recovered capacity.
- ❑ Appointed or disqualified a surrogate health care decision-maker (also may be oral or written).

Further, the doctor should ask for any written directives or instructions you have and put a copy in your medical record. Because of these recording requirements, keeping your medical record updated and readily available is very important.

People other than you may also orally inform the doctor of several things, such as disagreement among family members about a health care decision. Other health care providers are supposed to tell the doctor if they hear you revoke an advance health care directive, disqualify a surrogate, and or challenge a determination that you lack capacity.

---

[6]Remember that in addition to oral health care instructions, UHCDA allows you to orally inform the doctor of several things: (1) if you have capacity, revoking the appointment of an agent for health care decision-making or revoking all or part of an advance health care directive; (2) if you have capacity, appointing a surrogate health care decision-maker; and (3) disqualifying another from acting as surrogate (you do not need capacity to do this).

For example, if a nurse hears you say that you do not want X to act as a surrogate, the nurse should inform the doctor of this disqualification. The doctor must then record this information in your medical record and honor your instructions.

Exceptions to Following Your Wishes

Health care providers may decline to comply with the patient's or decision-maker's instructions **only** under two exceptions:

(1) **reasons of conscience**, if the instruction or decision is contrary to institutional policy expressly based on reasons of conscience **and** if the policy was timely communicated to you or your decision-maker; or

(2) if the instruction or decision would require **medically ineffective health care** or health care contrary to generally accepted health care standards. "Medically ineffective" means treatment that would not offer you any significant benefit, as determined by a doctor.

Providers or institutions that decline to comply must:

❑ Promptly inform you and your decision-maker.
❑ Provide continuing care to you until a transfer is made.
❑ Assist in making the transfer to a provider who will comply, unless you refuse such help.

What if the Doctor Refuses to Honor My Wishes?

Sometimes a family member will object to discontinuing life support for a terminally ill or comatose patient. Some people cannot let go of loved ones and hope for a miracle or a change for the better. Others may want to continue life support even though the patient does not want it. Still others may honor a patient's wish to continue life support even if the health care provider thinks such support is medically ineffective.

The terminally ill or comatose patient may have valid written health care directives or may have given oral instructions, which the doctor should honor. Yet, despite New Mexico laws that protect them, hospitals and doctors are sometimes afraid of being sued by a family member for the death of the ill person.

Even though UHCDA requires the doctor to transfer the patient to another physician, this does not address the real issue of lawsuits by family members. A doctor may be unwilling to honor an instruction if the doctor thinks the patient's family may sue. It is unlikely that a family who sued the hospital or doctor for honoring a valid instruction would win. But even defending the hospital or doctor in court is expensive. Rather than risk a lawsuit, the hospital or doctor may refuse to disconnect a patient from a machine or tube.

Yet the refusal to disconnect a patient could also result in a lawsuit. Family members could sue to force the hospital or doctor to honor the patient's wishes. Hospitals, nursing homes and doctors that refuse to honor a patient's wishes to terminate life support have been sued successfully in other states for **failing** to honor those wishes.

Talking with your doctor and family ahead of time can help prevent these problems. Putting your wishes in writing should help prevent future disputes. Ask your family to honor your wishes, even if your wishes are not what the family members would want for themselves. If your doctor is reluctant to honor your choices, consider finding a doctor who will.

Health Care Decisions for a Minor Child

UHCDA contains provisions for **minor** (under the age of fifteen[7]) children. Generally, a parent or guardian of an unemancipated minor can make health care decisions, including end-of-life decisions, for that minor. UHCDA gives certain minor children the right to make their own decisions about withholding or

---

[7]This age is a mistake in the law, which should be amended by the legislature. The age should be eighteen, unless the minor is emancipated (that is, someone between the ages of sixteen and eighteen who has been married, who is on active duty in the armed forces or who has been declared emancipated by court order).

withdrawing life-sustaining treatment. Two qualified health care professionals must first find the minor to have the mental and emotional capacity to do so. If there is disagreement about whether to withhold or withdraw life-sustaining treatment, the parties can go to court.

Determining Capacity

Patients are presumed to have capacity to make health care decisions, create health care directives and appoint a surrogate decision-maker. Patients can disqualify a surrogate at any time regardless of capacity. Unless otherwise specified in a written advance health care directive, **two** qualified health care professionals must determine a patient's lack of capacity.

One of these must be the primary physician, but the second does NOT have to be a physician. UHCDA defines qualified health care professional as "a health-care provider who is a physician, physician assistant, nurse practitioner, nurse, psychologist or social worker." If mental illness or developmental disability is involved, one of the qualified health care professionals must have training and expertise to assess functional impairment.

Failure to follow the doctor's treatment recommendations is not, on its own, evidence of incapacity. **UHCDA obligates primary physicians to document the determination of lack of capacity or recovery of capacity in the patient's health care record.** The primary physician must also inform the patient and authorized decision-maker about determinations of incapacity.

If at any time a patient challenges the determination of lack of capacity, the challenge prevails unless a court rules otherwise.

Legal Consequences of UHCDA

UHCDA contains immunities for providers and institutions that act in good faith and in accordance with generally accepted health care standards. Providers should not be subject to liability or discipline for complying with your instructions, no matter what your instructions are.

Providers or institutions that intentionally violate UHCDA are subject to liability for damages of up to $5,000 or actual damages, whichever is greater, plus reasonable attorney fees. Individuals who intentionally falsify, forge or conceal documents or evidence relating to a patient's wishes are similarly liable. These damages are in addition to other types of relief available under other criminal and civil laws.

Miscellaneous Provisions of UHCDA

UHCDA does not authorize agents or surrogates to consent to the admission of an individual to a mental health care facility. Other areas of New Mexico law cover these procedures. Nor does UHCDA affect other New Mexico laws that govern treatment for mental illness of an individual involuntarily committed to a mental health care institution. Finally, anyone interested in the patient's welfare, including a health care provider or institution, has the right to petition the state district court to stop or start a health care decision.

The Right to Die in New Mexico

The 1997 legislature significantly amended New Mexico's Uniform Health Care Decisions Act (UHCDA). In doing so, the legislature repealed New Mexico's Right to Die Act, effective July 1, 1997. But you **still** have the right to die. You **still** have the right to decline medical treatment and to die naturally.

Although the Right to Die Act is repealed, UHCDA allows an individual or the individual's decision-maker to make health care decisions "relating to life-sustaining treatment, including withholding or withdrawing life-sustaining treatment and the termination of life support; and directions to provide, withhold or withdraw artificial nutrition and hydration and all other forms of health care." UHCDA defines "life-sustaining treatment" as "any medical treatment or procedure without which the individual is likely to die within a relatively short time, as determined to a reasonable degree of medical certainty by the primary physician."

Some believed that New Mexico's twenty-year-old Right to Die Act was too limited because it applied only when one was in an irreversible coma or suffered from a terminal illness. The newer UHCDA offers individuals a broader range of choices because it covers **all** health care decisions, including end-of-life decisions. Those who do not desire life support should tell their families and doctors. Those who desire life support should also make their wishes known to their doctors and the people who will be making decisions for them if they become incapacitated. Making written instructions should avoid numerous and prolonged court battles like those in the Terri Schiavo case in Florida.

Many people feel strongly that they do not want to be connected to respirators, kidney machines or other life-support equipment if they are in a coma or terminally ill. Whether or not a person wants food and water[8] artificially given is a more difficult decision. Food and water can be given intravenously through a tube inserted in the arm, through a larger tube inserted in the nose or through a tube surgically implanted in the stomach. If someone is terminally ill or comatose, life-prolonging measures may unnecessarily prolong the patient's suffering. On the other hand, people do not like to think of themselves or their loved ones dying without food and water. Writing your preferences is recommended.

You may want to receive no treatment, including artificial nutrition and hydration, except for pain medicine. You may not want to be connected to machines, but may wish to receive artificial nutrition and hydration. Or you may want water, but not food, for a certain amount of time. Another issue to consider is whether you want artificial respiration (for breathing). Whatever choices are made, end-of-life instructions should include a statement that you **do** want medicine to reduce any pain or discomfort you may experience.

---

[8]The technical terms for medically-provided food and water are artificial nutrition and hydration. Some health care forms contain these terms rather than the words "food" and "water."

What if family members do not agree on what kind of treatment a patient would want? Doctors may be reluctant to withhold life-sustaining treatment if conflict exists. If the patient is capacitated and able to communicate with the doctor, the doctor should follow the patient's wishes. The hospital ethics committee[9] could convene to consult about the situation. The hospital ethics committee would **assist** in the decision-making process but would not make the decision for the patient. The committee and doctor would meet with the agent, surrogate or guardian, family members and others to understand the wishes and best interests of the patient.

What About My Old Living Will and Power of Attorney?

Before its repeal, New Mexico's Right to Die law allowed a competent person eighteen years or older to execute a document called a **living will** or **right to die statement**. This document directed that if a person was ever certified in writing by two physicians, one of whom was the attending physician, to be suffering from a terminal illness or irreversible coma, then maintenance medical treatment should not be used to prolong life. In other words, a person set out his or her wish to die naturally without life support.

Is your old living will still valid? What about your old durable power of attorney form? Yes to both! UHCDA says that any advance health care directive is valid if it complies with the provisions of UHCDA, "regardless of when or where executed or communicated." Guardianships, living wills, durable powers of attorney, and other advance directives for health care created before UHCDA became effective (July 1, 1995) should be

---

[9]Most hospitals have ethics committees that include some or all of the following members: medical staff, attorneys, clergy, ethicists (people who consider the moral and philosophical implications of choices), hospital administrators and representatives from the community.

honored. New powers of attorney and other health care directives should also be honored.

Although the law does not require you to update documents that express your wishes about health care, you may wish to do so. Review documents every few years to make sure they still accurately reflect your wishes. Appendix 1—Resources contains information about ordering selected forms.

Advance Directives from Another State

UHCDA contains a section about advance directives, durable powers of attorney, living wills, and similar documents created in other states. If the document complied with the laws of that state, New Mexico will usually honor it.

One exception might be Oregon's assisted suicide directives. Although Oregon allows an individual to authorize physician-assisted suicide through a written document, New Mexico does not allow physician-assisted suicide. New Mexico would not honor an Oregon directive authorizing physician-assisted suicide.

EMS "Do Not Resuscitate" Regulations

Health care providers, other than doctors, also are recognizing a person's right to refuse medical treatment. Emergency Medical Service (EMS) personnel who show up at your door when you call 911 for a medical emergency are subject to regulations that allow you to refuse resuscitation under certain circumstances.

With more and more people signing powers of attorney for health care, some have expressed concern about receiving medical care against their wishes. Previously when you called 911 and the ambulance arrived, the paramedics would attempt to resuscitate you, even if your health care agent was there with a copy of your health care power of attorney or living will.

The New Mexico Department of Health has created regulations that govern EMS advance directives. These regulations, which are updated periodically, help ensure that a patient's wishes will be honored. You may do one of two things (or both of them): (1) you can sign a health care power of attorney (POA) designating an individual to make health care decisions for you (this individual should know your feelings about resuscitation), or (2) your doctor can create an "EMS Do Not Resuscitate (DNR) Order," also signed by you, which directs that you not be resuscitated. If you are too sick to give consent to such an order, your health care decision-maker can ask for one IF that is what you would have wanted. You have the option of wearing an EMS bracelet that indicates you have an EMS DNR Order.

EMS DNR forms have no expiration date. You may revoke these documents at any time by destroying them in various ways (burning, tearing, etc.).

The regulations state that "EMS personnel shall follow EMS DNR Orders or Durable Powers of Attorney when encountering persons in pre-hospital settings." They must first verify your identity and the existence of a current EMS DNR Order or POA. If EMS personnel can't find the POA or EMS DNR Order, they will resuscitate you. So merely creating a document isn't good enough. Tell your family and friends you have the documents and tell them where to find the original documents. Store the Order in the EMS DNR envelope with bright red stripes so EMS personnel can recognize it. Keep it plainly visible by your bed or on your refrigerator. Have your doctor put copies in your medical file. The regulations don't say whether EMS personnel can accept photocopies of the signed documents, but this would probably be acceptable. Appendix 1—Resources contains information about how to obtain an EMS-DNR form.

Some people want to be resuscitated no matter what their prognosis is. If you want to be resuscitated, then you should instruct your health care decision-maker of your wishes, and you should **not** ask your doctor for an EMS DNR Order.

Summary of Health Care Decision-Making Options

A person now has five ways to express his or her wishes about health care decisions.

❑ Durable power of attorney for health care.
❑ UHCDA optional form.
❑ Emergency Medical Service-Do Not Resuscitate (EMS-DNR) form.
❑ Any other form that complies with UHCDA.
❑ Give oral instructions and/or orally appoint a surrogate.

UHCDA should result in fewer families having to go to court to obtain a guardianship over an incapacitated person. However, if families are disputing who should serve as decision-maker or what the decision should be, a guardianship proceeding may still be necessary.

UHCDA is intended to promote an individual's autonomy in making health care decisions. Although a surrogate health care decision-maker can now be appointed orally or just assume authority over an incapacitated patient, it is still wise to put your wishes about your health care in writing. You have the right to appoint whomever you wish to serve as your agent under a health care power of attorney. You have the right to seek or refuse medical treatment. You have the right to give instructions about end-of-life decisions. Whatever your philosophy of health care is, putting your wishes in writing gives you a better chance that your instructions will be followed and that conflicts between family members will be avoided.

Powers of attorney for health care created before or after UHCDA should be valid. Powers of attorney are effective until revocation or death, no matter when signed (i.e., old powers of attorney remain effective unless revoked). Living wills created before or after UHCDA should also be valid. Even an invalidly executed living will or other advance directive is a "written instruction" that should be honored under UHCDA.

Facilities that receive Medicare/Medicaid funding have a duty under the federal Patient Self-Determination Act to ask whether patients have signed powers of attorney, living wills or other advance directives. UHCDA provides another layer of options for

New Mexicans making health care decisions and additional obligations for health care providers.

No Constitutional Right to Assisted Suicide

Society accepts that a competent adult has the right to decline medical treatment, whether or not the person is terminally ill. Asking for help in dying is more controversial.

On June 26, 1997 the U.S. Supreme Court, in two separate cases, ruled that terminally ill, competent adults do **not** have a constitutional right to physician-assisted suicide. In 1995 two lower federal courts affirmed, on different constitutional grounds, the right of certain individuals to seek help in ending their lives. The Supreme Court reversed both cases.

In one case, the lower court found no difference between allowing one patient to refuse or end lifesaving medical treatment and another patient to ask for help in dying (such as a prescription of pills to cause death). The Supreme Court found a big difference, stating, "[W]hen a patient refuses life sustaining medical treatment, he dies from an underlying disease or pathology; but if a patient ingests lethal medication prescribed by a physician, he is killed by that medication."

Therefore, the Court ruled that it is acceptable to allow one person the right to refuse unwanted medical treatment and not allow another the right to physician-assisted suicide. Making such a distinction does not violate constitutional equal protection rights. The Supreme Court noted that a doctor can provide painkilling drugs that hasten a patient's death if the physician's purpose and intent is to ease the patient's pain, rather than cause the patient's death.

In the second case, the Supreme Court ruled that individuals do not have a constitutionally protected liberty interest to commit physician-assisted suicide. The U.S. Constitution protects certain fundamental rights and liberties that are "deeply rooted in this Nation's history and tradition." Physician-assisted suicide, concluded the Court, is not one of these rights. To so decide would require the Court to "reverse centuries of legal doctrine and practice, and strike down the considered policy of almost every State [banning assisted suicide]."

The Supreme Court did not totally close the door on the notion of physician-assisted suicide. A footnote states that the Court's ruling "does not foreclose the possibility that some applications of the [law] may impose an intolerable intrusion on the patient's freedom." To persuade the Court that an assisted suicide ban is unconstitutional, a person would have to present to the Court "considerably stronger arguments" than those in the present case.

Although citizens do not have a constitutional right to physician-assisted suicide, individual states are still free to pass their own laws on this subject.

New Mexico Law Does Not Allow Assisted Suicide

New Mexico's criminal laws include a law that states, "Assisting suicide consists of deliberately aiding another in the taking of his own life. Whoever commits assisting suicide is guilty of a fourth degree felony." This law would apply to doctors, spouses and others who help anyone commit suicide, regardless of how much a person is suffering or wants to die. In New Mexico anyone who is found guilty of helping someone to commit suicide may face a prison term.

While deliberately helping someone commit suicide is illegal in New Mexico, declining life support or artificial nutrition and hydration is not suicide under our law.

Does Signing a Health Care Directive Affect My Life Insurance?

Under UHCDA life insurance companies cannot refuse to insure a person simply because that person has signed (or not signed) a health care directive. The law also provides that signing such documents does not invalidate or modify an existing life insurance policy.

While many individuals do not want to be connected to machines if they are seriously ill, others want to live as long as possible, with or without machines. UHCDA further states that insurers **cannot** require a person to sign advance health care directives in order to be insured.

Individuals who do **not** want life-sustaining treatment may worry that their beneficiaries will be unable to collect life insurance benefits if they refuse treatment. To make sure that life insurance policies will pay off if someone refuses treatment and dies as a result, UHCDA includes a provision that states, "Death resulting from the withholding or withdrawal of health care. . . does not for any purpose constitute a suicide, a homicide or other crime. . . ."

More and more people are recognizing the importance of planning ahead for health care decisions. Having a health care power of attorney and written instructions about your health care wishes should help ensure that your wishes regarding medical treatment and care are followed by your health care decision-makers.

RE: Chapter 3 of this book, updated nursing home figures are available on our web site:

www.abogadapress.com

or send $1.00 + self-addressed, stamped envelope requesting the 2006 **Life Planning** Supplement to 2004 edition of book to Abogada Press, POB 36011, Albuquerque NM 87176.

Thank you!

3

PLANNING FOR NURSING HOME CARE

Many older people fear that one day they will require nursing home care. Currently, in New Mexico, the cost of nursing home care ranges from $3,500 to $6,000 or more **per month**. What if a person cannot afford nursing home care? Must a couple sell everything to pay for nursing home care? Are any benefits available to pay for nursing home care? Does Medicare pay for nursing home care? How can people protect their assets if they need nursing home care?

Some people may have loved ones who already reside in a nursing home. Others may anticipate requiring nursing home care in the future. New Mexicans need to know how to qualify for public funds to assist them in meeting the cost of nursing home care.

Sometimes a couple has saved their money throughout their lives, only to see their savings dwindle to pay for nursing home care. In the past if one spouse required nursing home care, the at-home spouse had to exhaust the couple's savings and in some instances sell the home to pay for the cost of nursing home care. The at-home spouse was left with little to live on. The term **spousal impoverishment** was created to describe this situation.

In response to widespread national concern about spousal impoverishment, the U.S. Congress passed laws that provide some protection for couples. New Mexico also passed laws that allow the at-home spouse to keep certain resources, while still allowing the ill spouse to qualify for assistance for nursing home care. New Mexico law also allows some of the resources of an **unmarried individual** to be protected.

Choosing a Nursing Home

Choosing a nursing home is difficult, but more information is now available to help. AARP publishes a guide listed in Appendix 1—Resources. The New Mexico Long Term Care Ombudsman Program, through the New Mexico Aging and Long-Term Services Department, has published a Guide to New Mexico Nursing Homes. The guide lists eighty-two licensed and federally certified New Mexico nursing homes with information about residents, costs and state inspections and surveys. Guides for several regions of New Mexico are available from your local Ombudsman Program, library or senior center. Call the New Mexico Aging and Long-Term Services Department Ombudsman Program, 1-800-432-2080, if you cannot locate a guide.

What Programs Will Pay for Nursing Home Care?

At age sixty-five many Americans become eligible for **Medicare** benefits. Medicare is a federal health insurance program available to individuals who **receive Social Security benefits** and are at least age sixty-five or disabled. Many people think that Medicare will pay for nursing home care. **Medicare, however, will only pay for up to 100 days of** *skilled* **nursing home care.**[1] Most nursing home residents receive only intermediate or custodial care, which Medicare will not cover **at all**. Also, individuals who receive benefits for the 100 days of skilled care must make a **co-payment** after receiving benefits for twenty days.[2] Most traditional

---

[1]Medicare will, however, pay for some home health care and hospice care expenses.

[2]The Income Support Division of the state Human Services Department (ISD) administers the Qualified Medicare Beneficiary (QMB) program, which pays the Medicare monthly premium, deductibles and co-insurance for certain qualified, low-income individuals. Income and resource limitations apply; these change during the second half of each year. Contact the Human Services Department, 1-888-997-2583, for current figures. Individuals receiving

health care policies also do **not** cover long-term care in a nursing home.

Note: One positive aspect of paying privately for nursing home care is that expenses for long term care, including personal care, for chronically ill individuals are deductible as medical expenses on the individual's income tax return. Consult a tax attorney or CPA to determine if this deduction applies to you.

When someone who needs nursing home care[3] runs out of money, the person can apply for **Medicaid**, which provides funds to assist individuals in meeting the cost of nursing home care. Medicaid is a program, managed by the **state**, that provides money to reimburse certain health care costs of indigent people. In New Mexico about 70% of every Medicaid dollar spent is federal money, and the remainder is state money.

Many people think of Medicaid as a benefits program for only very poor or disabled people. However, Medicaid **also** provides funds to supplement nursing home costs through its Institutional Medical Assistance Program. In New Mexico this program is called **Medical Assistance for Persons Requiring Institutional Care** (called nursing home benefits or NHB in the rest of this chapter). The NHB program is a public benefits program that spends Medicaid dollars to pay for nursing home care and certain rehabilitation and hospital care for elderly and handicapped individuals. In addition, the NHB program may pay for residence in a shelter care home, boarding home or assisted living facility. However, there is a waiting list for these services. The NHB

Medicare Part A benefits who meet the income and resource limits may apply to ISD for QMB, SLIMB, and QI-1 benefits. The New Mexico Aging and Long-Term Services Department HIBAC Program, 1-800-432-2080, can also provide information.

[3]Alternatives to nursing home care exist. Shelter care homes, boarding homes and assisted living facilities can help residents dress, bathe, shop, eat, get to appointments, take medicines, etc. Costs of such facilities range from $2,000 to $4,000 a month. Medicare does not cover these expenses, although some long-term care insurance may. Medicaid may cover these expenses through a waiver program, but there is currently a six-month to 24-month waiting list.

program will **not** pay for care for most individuals who wish to remain in the home.[4]

Each state's NHB program eligibility requirements vary. New Mexico participates in the NHB program. The New Mexico Human Services Department (HSD) administers the NHB program.[5] This chapter of the book will discuss **New Mexico's** eligibility requirements for the NHB program.

Eligibility for NHB—Generally

For those who wish to apply for the NHB program, contact your local Income Support Division, Human Services Department office. To be eligible for the NHB program in New Mexico, the applicant: (1) must be a New Mexico resident and have been residing in a nursing home for at least thirty days; **note:** only residents of licensed nursing homes are eligible for NHB; (2) must be sixty-five years old, blind or disabled and have a medical condition that **requires** nursing home care; (3) must have a gross monthly income of $1,692[6] (for 2004) or less; (4) must have no

---

[4]Some individuals may qualify for Coordinated Community In-Home Care (CCIC) benefits, which help pay for nursing care in the individual's home. The CCIC program is very small and there is a long waiting list. Contact the Income Support Division, Human Services Department, in your county for more information on CCIC benefits, or call the toll-free line for Human Services, 1-888-997-2583. The New Mexico Aging and Long-Term Services Department's HIBAC Program may also help, 1-800-432-2080.

[5]You may order a copy of the Human Services Department's Medical Assistance Division's Program Manual, an inch-thick document that contains the state rules and regulations governing New Mexico's NHB program. This manual is highly technical and probably contains far more information than most people would want to know about the NHB program. Copies of the most recent manual on the Medical Assistance for Persons Requiring Institutional Care may be ordered from: Human Services Department, Medical Assistance Division, P.O. Box 2348, Santa Fe, NM 87504-2348, or by calling 827-3100 (in Santa Fe) or 1-888-997-2583. Ask for the current cost of the document before ordering.

[6]The actual gross monthly income limit is $1,672 but HSD disregards the first $20 of income. The ultimate effect of this regulation is that the income limit is $1,692. This chapter will use the $1,692 figure throughout.

more than $2,000 in personal resources (bank account, real estate, stocks or other personal resources); and (5) may have a burial account containing $1,500 (the applicant may also own a cemetery plot, a prepaid burial space, or a prepaid burial plan). The $2,000 in personal resources cannot earn interest, but the $1,500 burial account may earn interest if the burial account is kept separate from other resources. The applicant can have a **term** life insurance policy, but an insurance policy with a cash value is counted as a resource.

Eligibility for NHB—Income Limits, Single Applicants

Federal law allows states to set certain eligibility limits, based on income and resources, for applicants who seek NHB. New Mexico requires individuals to have a gross monthly income of $1,692 or less (for 2004).[7] Federal law does allow a state to adopt a **lower** income eligibility limit, and New Mexico used to do so. But in 1999 New Mexico raised its income eligibility cap significantly in accordance with federal guidelines. For applicants whose gross monthly income exceeds $1,692, creating an income diversion trust (discussed on page 85) might enable them to become eligible for NHB. Without such a trust a single applicant with over $1,692 in income could not receive NHB. *Income* includes social security benefits, pension benefits, interest and dividends earned on investments and other income.[8]

Eligibility for NHB—Income Limits, Married Applicants

This chapter will refer to the spouse who requires nursing home care as the **ill spouse** or **applicant**. NHB regulations actually

---

[7]This income amount changes on January 1 of each year. Contact your local Income Support Division, Human Services Department office for an update.

[8]Remember that all sources of income, not just social security benefits, must be counted. This would include income from rental properties and annuities.

call the ill spouse the **institutionalized spouse**, but "ill spouse" is easier to read. This chapter will refer to the spouse who does not require nursing home care as the **at-home spouse**. NHB regulations actually call the at-home spouse the "community spouse" and the term "community spouse" may be used interchangeably in this chapter with the term "at-home spouse."

As mentioned above, an applicant may only have $1,692 gross monthly income to be eligible for NHB. To determine the income eligibility of married applicants for the NHB program, the Human Services Department (HSD) uses one of two methods. The first method examines the applicant's income that is in his or her own name. (HSD looks at the name on the check or other source of income. If it has both names, it will be considered to be owned one-half to each spouse.) If the applicant's own income is $1,692 or less, HSD ignores the other spouse's income. The applicant is eligible for NHB if the applicant also meets the resource requirements.

If the applicant's own income is greater than $1,692, HSD uses a second method. New Mexico is a **community property** state. Under community property principles all property acquired or income earned during the marriage is considered to be owned half by one spouse and half by the other spouse, no matter who actually earned it. (Gifts and inheritances acquired by one spouse during the marriage and property acquired before the marriage are the separate property of the individual who received it.) Using this principle, HSD divides the couple's **total** gross income in half. If the applicant's one-half is below $1,692, then the applicant is eligible for the NHB program, *assuming the couple's **resources** do not exceed allowable limits*. Federal and state law allows certain transfers of the home and other resources to the at-home spouse in order for the ill spouse to become eligible for the NHB program (transfers discussed on page 67).

Example 1: Husband requires nursing home care. Husband's income is $1,050/month. Wife's income is $2,000 a month. Under method number one, HSD will look first to husband's income.

Because his income is less than the $1,692 limit, husband's income qualifies him for NHB. HSD will then examine the couple's resources.

Example 2: Wife requires nursing home care. Wife's income is $1,700/month. Husband's income is $300/month. Under method number two, HSD will add the two incomes together and divide by two ($1,700 + $300 = $2,000 ÷ 2 = $1,000/month income attributed to each spouse). Wife meets the income eligibility requirements for the NHB program. HSD will then examine the couple's resources.

Example 3: Husband requires nursing home care. Husband's income is $2,400/month from Social Security benefits and a pension. Wife's income is $1,200/month from investment income. The couple's total monthly income is $3,600. Dividing their total monthly income by two, HSD considers each spouse to have $1,800/month in income. This amount exceeds the $1,692/month limit. Husband is not eligible to apply for NHB without legal action, such as a court-ordered division of income or property, discussed on page 86, or income diversion trust, discussed on page 85.

Special New Mexico Laws Re: Income from ERA and PERA Pension Benefits

Normally, if applicants for any Medicaid benefits decline income to which they are entitled, they are forever barred from receiving benefits. In response to this harsh result, the New Mexico Legislature passed a law, called the New Mexico Retired Teacher's Act, that exempts income received from a teacher's retirement pension, the Educational Retirement Association (ERA). The law states that if the income received by the retired teacher will make the teacher ineligible for certain benefits (such as NHB), the pension administrator can decrease the amount of pension benefits so that the retired teacher then becomes eligible for the other benefits. This law applies **only** to ERA benefits. Another law allows Public Employees Retirement Association (PERA) benefits to be reduced under certain circumstances.

Eligibility for NHB—Resources, Single Applicants

Assuming their income meets HSD standards, individuals whose **countable resources** do not exceed $2,000 are eligible for the NHB program. Countable resources are any resources that the individual has the right to liquidate unless specifically excluded in the state regulations. For single applicants, countable resources include the home unless certain exceptions apply (see Chart 1 on page 62), bank accounts, stocks, bonds, vacant lots, IOUs, real estate contracts and other resources. The applicant can also have up to $1,500 for burial purposes. This money, if kept separate, can earn interest.

An HSD regulation allows a "fully paid irrevocably assigned insurance policy payable to the funeral home" to pay for specified burial services and items **for any amount** to be excluded as a resource. This means an individual can purchase an irrevocable insurance policy for a predetermined amount to cover funeral costs and name a funeral home as the beneficiary. If done properly, HSD would not count the policy as a resource, even if it were for an amount larger than $1,500. Depending on the allocation in the burial contract between burial space items and services, an individual might also be able to set aside burial funds up to $1,500 in a separate account.

HSD always makes the resource determination as of the first moment of the first day of the month. The applicant is ineligible for any month in which the countable resources exceed the current resource standard. This means that if the value of the applicant's resources increases over $2,000 due to earning interest or appreciating, the applicant will not be eligible for NHB.

Unless a single person meets one of the exceptions listed in Chart 1, the home will be considered a resource. An absence of more than six months indicates that the home may no longer serve as the principal place of residence. If the applicant states a

subjective intent, reasonable or not, to return home, the home will not be counted as a resource.[9] If the applicant does not intend to return home, in most instances the home must be sold at fair market value and the proceeds spent down to the resource limits discussed above.

---

[9]In the past HSD required this subjective intent to be reasonable. That regulation conflicted with federal law, which states that the applicant's subjective intent is all that is required, and HSD has now adopted a regulation that says if a person states a subjective intent to return home, even if that intent is unreasonable, HSD will not count the home as a resource.

Chart 1

Single Applicants, Resource Summary

Not Counted (Excluded)	Counted
$2,000 in resources that cannot earn interest.	Home, unless (1) applicant intends to return home, or (2) dependent relative has resided in home and continues to reside in home, or (3) someone else owns the home as a joint tenant with the applicant and refuses to sell his or her share.
$1,500 in burial account that can earn interest and/or prepaid burial plot.	Resources over $2,000 in value, (including automobile in some cases).
The value of wedding and engagement rings. HSD regulations state that the value of personal effects is included, but in practice HSD usually does not count personal effects.	Automobile, unless used for transportation for medical treatment, contains special equipment for a disabled person or is necessary for employment.
Term life insurance.	Pro rata share of joint accounts.
Life insurance policies if total cumulative face value of policies does not exceed $1,500 or irrevocable policies.	
Vehicle required to obtain treatment of specific, persistent or recurring medical problem or equipped with special device for disability.	

Eligibility for NHB—Resources, Married Applicants

As with a single applicant, a married applicant may have no more than $2,000 in resources, an irrevocable funeral policy, and $1,500 in a burial account. However, the ill spouse is allowed by federal and New Mexico law to transfer certain resources to the at-home spouse, discussed in detail beginning on page 67. Also, HSD does not count certain resources when determining eligibility for a married applicant (see Chart 2).

HSD determines the amount of a couple's resources by conducting an assessment of the resources. The applicant or spouse must provide all financial information requested by HSD. HSD caseworkers should help the couple calculate the amount of resources that must be spent on nursing home care before the ill spouse is eligible for NHB and the amount of resources that can be protected for the at-home spouse.

The next sections of this chapter will discuss the transfer-of-resources rules and spousal-impoverishment laws enacted by Congress and HSD.

NOTE: **Remember that resource eligibility amounts and other amounts change yearly. Transfer rules and eligibility amounts are covered by very complex HSD regulations. Contact your local HSD office or a knowledgeable attorney to help you through the process.**

Chart 2	
Married Applicant and Spouse, Resource Summary	
Not Counted (Excluded)	*Counted*
Home (but see discussion on page 78).	
One car, no matter how new or nice.	
Personal property, such as furniture, appliances, clothing, jewelry, etc.	
The **greater** of $31,290 or one-half of the couple's total resources up to $92,760 (discussed in detail on page 76).	Assets over $92,760.
$2,000 in resources that **cannot** earn interest.	
$1,500 in burial account that **can** earn interest, and/or irrevocable funeral insurance policy.	
Term life insurance.	
Prepaid burial plot.	

Penalties for Transfer of Resources

In 1988 Congress passed the Medicare Catastrophic Coverage Act (MCCA) that contains provisions concerning the Medicaid program for people who require nursing home care. New Mexico's regulations on NHB include the transfer-of-resources penalties - created by federal law.

With a few exceptions, transferring resources for less than fair market value in order to qualify for NHB will result in a period during which the applicant is ineligible to receive NHB for nursing home care. Transfers of resources that take place **within 36 months** of application for NHB (otherwise referred to as a "look-back period"), except between spouses, are penalized.[10] The look-back period is **within 60 months** for certain transfers to or from a trust.

The penalty period runs from the date the resource was transferred. If the transfer occurred within 36 months of the NHB application, the penalty equals the total uncompensated value of the transferred resources divided by the average monthly cost to a private patient of nursing facility services ($3,899 for applications made on or after January 1, 2004).

Example 1: Mary, a single woman, gave her home worth $60,000 (her only resource) to her friend Samantha, on April 1. There will be a 15-month penalty period from the date of the transfer ($60,000 ÷ $3,899 = 15.39; HSD regulations allow the fraction to be dropped). Mary does not enter a nursing home until 8 months later. She will not be eligible for NHB for 7 more months.

Example 2: Mary, a single woman, transfers her entire $200,000 estate to family and friends on January 1, 2001 and a few days later enters the nursing home.[11] Applying the formula

---

[10]If you do not apply for NHB until at least 37 months after a transfer (no matter how large or small) is made, the transfer would not have to be reported to HSD when applying for NHB.

[11]The intent of the current federal transfer penalty laws is to discourage transferring one's entire estate to friends and family. Many people would be reluctant to do this anyway, and under the current law Mary would have to pay

($200,000 ÷ $3,899), the resulting penalty period is 51 months, over four years. Mary will not be eligible for NHB until January 1, 2004, as long as she does not make her application for NHB until that time.

Example 3: Mary transfers her house on September 1, 2001. She enters the nursing home on November 1, 2004, 38 months later, and applies for NHB benefits. Under current transfer laws, Mary is not subject to any transfer penalties because the transfer occurred more than 36 months before her NHB application.

Exceptions to Transfer-of-Resources Penalties

Congress created exceptions to the transfer-of-resources penalties. Federal **and** state regulations allow the following transfers **without triggering a penalty period**:

Transferring the applicant's home to: (1) a spouse, (2) a minor, blind or disabled child, (3) a sibling who has an equity interest in the home and who resided in the home for at least one year prior to the applicant's admission to the nursing home, and (4) a child who resided in the home for at least two years prior to the applicant's admission to the nursing home and who provided care enabling the applicant to reside at home rather than in a nursing home for that two-year time period.

In addition, there is no transfer penalty for the transfer of other assets to a blind or disabled child or to certain trusts for a blind or disabled child.

Transferring resources other than as stated above are permitted only if the applicant shows through objective evidence that: (1) the applicant intended to dispose of the resource either at fair market value or for other valuable consideration, (2) the resources were transferred exclusively for a purpose other than to qualify for

---

privately for care for almost 5 years as a result of the transfers she made. People who consider giving away a large amount of assets in order to become eligible for NHB should strongly consider the ethical and financial aspects of such an action.

NHB, and (3) the denial of eligibility would work an undue hardship.

To determine if undue hardship exists, HSD will consider whether the transfer was made to a non-family member, whether the applicant can present convincing evidence that every effort was made to recover the transferred resource, and whether it is verified that the applicant cannot obtain care in any long-term-care facility in the state without Medicaid coverage, including state-run facilities. If all three of these criteria are met, HSD can declare an undue hardship and find an applicant eligible for NHB. This third exception would be used most often in cases where third parties have exploited an applicant's resources and refuse to give back the resources.

Transferring Resources Back

If an applicant transferred a resource for less than fair market value, becoming eligible for NHB during the penalty period is possible. To do so, the transferred resource may be transferred back to the applicant and spent on the applicant's care until the applicant is eligible for NHB. Alternatively, the recipient of the resource may pay for the applicant's care in an amount equal to the uncompensated fair market value of the transferred resource.

Transfers Between Spouses and Others

An ill spouse is allowed to transfer certain resources, not including the home, to specified people. The U.S. Congress passed laws on this subject, and federal law governs New Mexico law. Current federal law states that the transfer penalty period does **not** apply if resources, other than the home, are transferred to any of the following:

❑ The community (at-home) spouse (or to another for the sole benefit of the individual's spouse) as long as the spouse does not transfer the resources to another person for less than fair market value.[12]

❑ Another for the sole benefit of the community spouse.

❑ The individual's minor, blind or disabled child.

❑ A trust for the sole benefit of a disabled individual under age 65.

Note that if resources are transferred to individuals other than the spouse or the other individuals listed above, penalties apply. This means you cannot give away your resources to your children or friends without incurring a penalty. Finally, just because HSD allows transfers of resources *between spouses* without imposing a penalty does not mean the at-home spouse can keep all of the resources. The limits on the amount of resources allowed to be eligible for NHB still apply.

New Mexico's regulations state that any transfers made by the at-home spouse *after October 1, 1990* are subject to the same penalties as transfers by the ill spouse. This may be true even if the transfer is made *after* the ill spouse is receiving Medicaid benefits. If HSD interprets this regulation to mean that after the at-home spouse has sole title to the home, a penalty will be incurred if the at-home spouse transfers the home for less than fair market value,[13] *including putting the title in joint tenancy with third parties.* The penalty period for such a transfer by an *at-home* spouse would run from the date of the transfer, regardless of how long the ill spouse had lived in the nursing home.[14] The penalty would affect the ill

---

[12]Federal law contains this exception, which New Mexico regulations omit. But states are bound by federal law, and so this exception should apply to New Mexicans.

[13]Federal tax law says that if a home is used by the taxpayer as the taxpayer's principal residence for 2 out of 5 years, the taxpayer can exclude up to $250,000 of capital gain ($500,000 for married individuals filing a joint income tax return) from the sale of this residence. One disadvantage of transferring the home to the children (if they did not live in the home) as a gift might be the loss of this tax benefit.

[14]HSD's general counsel has said a spouse can transfer assets after the ill spouse qualifies for NHB, but there is no written regulation that allows this.

spouse's eligibility for NHB for a period of time equal to the value of the resources transferred at less than fair market value divided by the average cost of nursing home care.

WARNING AND DISCLAIMER: In 1997 the U.S. Congress made it a crime for individuals to knowingly and willfully dispose of assets for NHB eligibility if disposing of assets resulted in a transfer penalty period. Congress <u>repealed</u> this law in August 1997 and substituted a provision making it a crime for anyone (including attorneys), for a fee, to knowingly and willfully counsel an individual to dispose of assets in order to become eligible for NHB if it results in the imposition of a penalty. This law was declared unconstitutional by the U.S. Attorney General who was serving at the time. Nevertheless, an attorney who is helping you with NHB questions may still ask you to sign a statement that the attorney did not counsel you to transfer assets. Likewise, the author is only providing information about NHB, not counseling anyone to transfer anything.

Chart 3
Summary of Transfers of Property

Resource Transferred	Before or After Entering Nursing Home?	To Whom Transfer Is Made	Penalty Imposed?
Home	Before or after	Spouse, dependent or disabled child, sibling with ownership rights or child who cared for parent (see page 78)	No
Home	Before or after	Children or others	Yes
Other resources	Before or after	Spouse (who **cannot** retransfer resources to others)	No
Other resources	Before or after	Children or others	Yes
Excluded resources, besides home	Before or after	Anyone	No

Avoiding Spousal Impoverishment

The following provisions will only help married couples.

The federal MCCA includes spousal-impoverishment provisions. As discussed in the introduction to this chapter, *spousal impoverishment* occurs when the at-home spouse is forced to spend all of the couple's resources and the ill spouse's income to pay for the ill spouse's nursing home care. As a result, the at-home spouse is often unable to stay in the home and is unable to maintain the standard of living for which the couple had worked so hard. Due to the inherent unfairness of this, Congress passed certain laws to help protect the at-home spouse from total impoverishment. The law protects a portion of the couple's income and resources for the at-home spouse.

Under federal law the at-home spouse is allowed a community spouse resource allowance (CSRA) and community spouse monthly income allowance (CSMIA) based on a formula. New Mexico's spousal-impoverishment regulations, based on the federal law, are detailed and hard to understand.

Community Spouse Monthly Income Allowance (CSMIA)

The CSMIA is the amount of **income** HSD will allow the at-home (community) spouse to keep if the ill spouse requires nursing home care. The goal of the laws on CSMIA is to allow the at-home spouse enough income to remain in the home and to enjoy a lifestyle similar to that which the couple has always enjoyed.

For 2004 the minimum CSMIA is $1,515/month (changes the middle of each year). If there are shelter needs in excess of $455 to a maximum of $804, then the maximum allowable CSMIA is $2,319/month. An administrative hearing officer or a court can order that the at-home spouse receive more than $2,319/month. The CSMIA figures change in July of each year.

As mentioned above, HSD will examine the couple's income and resources to determine if a married applicant is eligible for

NHB. For purposes of determining **eligibility**, HSD first examines the applicant's income. If the applicant's income is less than $1,692 (for 2004), HSD then examines the couple's resources. If the applicant's income is greater than $1,692, HSD applies community property principles, adds the couple's income and divides by two, no matter who earns the income. The applicant's one-half share of the income must be $1,692 or below. After HSD finds an applicant eligible for NHB, community property principles no longer apply (this concept is discussed in more detail on page 79).

If the applicant's income and resources qualify the applicant for NHB, HSD then looks to the CSMIA regulations to see how much income the at-home spouse can actually keep and how much must be spent on nursing home care. If the cost of the nursing home is more than the amount of income available to the ill spouse after applying CSMIA rules, NHB will pay the rest of the cost of the nursing home.

New Mexico's HSD regulations describe how to determine the amount of income the community spouse can retain. Federal law and New Mexico regulations also state that the at-home spouse is **not** required to contribute any portion of his or her own income to the ill spouse. The following examples illustrate how HSD will determine the at-home spouse's CSMIA share of the couple's income.

Note: In Examples 1-4, HSD may also deduct from the *ill spouse's* gross monthly income $66.60, which is the amount of the Medicare Part B premium for 2004. If the ill spouse is already receiving NHB monies (Medicaid benefits), HSD will not deduct this $66.60 because Medicaid and not the ill spouse is paying the premium. HSD may also allow certain other deductions for old non-covered medical bills.

Example 1

Ill spouse (husband)

$1,800	gross monthly income of husband
- 50	personal needs allowance[15]
- 1,315	income allowed to wife under CSMIA
$ 435	of husband's income will be paid to nursing home each month

At-home spouse (wife)

$ 200	gross monthly income[16] of wife
+1,315	from husband's income
$1,515	minimum CSMIA allowed to wife

If the at-home spouse has excess shelter needs (that is, if her shelter expenses exceed one-third of the CSMIA), the HSD case worker may increase the CSMIA up to $2,319. The at-home spouse may be entitled to **more than** $2,319 if an administrative hearing officer or a court so orders. One reason to increase the at-home spouse's share would be if the at-home spouse has excess medical needs.

The ill spouse's remaining income after allowable deductions (in this example, $435) must be paid to the nursing facility—that amount is called his *medical care credit*. NHB will pay the difference between the cost of care minus the medical care credit.

---

[15]HSD regulations mandate that the "institutionalized spouse is entitled to $50.00 for his/her personal needs before any other deductions are considered." New Mexico may increase this $50 allowance in the future.

[16]When the applicant first applied for NHB, HSD determined him to be eligible because the couple's total income, $1,800 ÷ 2 = $900, was less than the $1,692 limit on income.

Example 2

Ill spouse (husband)

$ 1150	gross monthly income of husband
- 50	personal needs allowance
- 615	income allowed to wife under CSMIA
$ 485	of husband's income will be paid to nursing home each month

At-home spouse (wife)

$ 900	gross monthly income of wife
+ 615	from husband's income
$1,515	minimum CSMIA allowed to wife

Example 3

Couple's gross monthly income is $1,515 or less.

If the couple's total gross monthly income is $1,515 or less, the ill (institutionalized) spouse is entitled to the $50 personal needs allowance and the at-home spouse retains the remaining income. In this example Medicaid would pay the entire cost of care. However, the government will not contribute money to the at-home spouse to bring the income up to the minimum CSMIA if the couple's income is less than $1,515.

Example 4

Ill spouse (wife)

$ 600	gross monthly income
- 50	personal needs allowance
$ 550	of wife's income will be paid to nursing home each month

At-home spouse (husband)
$1,600   gross monthly income of husband

In this example, the at-home spouse gets to keep the entire $1,600 and is not required to contribute any portion to the ill spouse. Nor must the ill spouse contribute any income to the at-home spouse unless ordered to do so by an administrative hearing officer or a court. The ill spouse's medical care credit would be $550 ($600 - $50 personal needs allowance = $550). NHB would pay the rest of the nursing home cost.

Example 5

Ill spouse (husband)
$3,500   gross monthly income of husband

At-home spouse (wife)
$1,700   gross monthly income of wife

This couple is not eligible for NHB because their total monthly income of $5,200 divided by two = $2,600, which exceeds the $1,692 allowed for NHB applicants. This couple could establish an income diversion trust for the ill spouse's income, or the couple would have to pay the entire amount of nursing home care until their resources were exhausted. Even if the couple exhausted their resources, the ill spouse would not be eligible for NHB because the couple's income is too high to qualify for benefits. A court-ordered division of property (and court-ordered reduction of husband's income) or divorce might help husband become eligible for NHB, as an alternative to an income diversion trust.

Community Spouse Resource Allowance (CSRA)

The at-home (community) spouse can keep a certain amount of the couple's resources. To determine the community spouse's resource allowance (CSRA), HSD will examine and assess the couple's resources **on the first day of the first month of continuous institutionalization of the ill spouse**. On that day HSD will take a "snapshot" of the couple's resources and calculate "the total value of the couple's countable resources [all resources that are not excluded as a resource] held both jointly or separately by the couple as of the first moment of the first day of the month one spouse became institutionalized for a continuous period of at least thirty (30) consecutive days beginning on or after September 30, 1989." Each spouse's share is one-half of the total value of the resources.[17]

After HSD performs the initial assessment of a couple's resources, the at-home spouse is entitled to keep a certain amount of the resources. HSD will calculate the CSRA from the spousal share. The spousal share is one-half of the couple's total countable resources. The CSRA equals the *greater* of the **state** minimum resource allowance (currently $31,290) or one-half of the couple's total countable resources held either jointly or separately up to the current federal maximum standard ($92,760 for 2004).[18] This computation of the spousal share occurs **only once** at the beginning of the first continuous period of institutionalization. If the at-home spouse acquires resources after HSD calculates the spousal share, HSD will not count the newly acquired resources.

---

[17]HSD divides the couple's total countable resources by two to determine the spousal shares.

[18]The federal maximum standard is indexed to the federal consumer price index and increases annually. The state minimum resource allowance has not changed since 1990.

Example 1: The total countable resources of a couple are $30,000. The CSRA equals the *greater* of the **state** minimum resource allowance ($31,290) or one-half of the couple's total countable resources up to $92,760 (in 2004). In this example one-half of the couple's total countable resources is $15,000. Applying the rule that the CSRA is the *greater* of $31,290 or $15,000, the entire $30,000 may be transferred to the at-home (community) spouse. The at-home spouse may keep the entire $30,000 (although the ill spouse is allowed to keep $2,000 in resources and the $1,500 in a burial account and still be eligible for NHB).

Example 2: The total countable resources of a couple are $150,000. The CSRA equals the *greater* of the **state** minimum resource allowance ($31,290) or one-half of the couple's total countable resources up to $92,760, here $75,000. Under this rule the total of $75,000 may be transferred to the at-home spouse because $75,000 is greater than $31,290. The remaining $75,000 owned by the couple must be spent on the ill spouse's care[19] until the ill spouse qualifies for NHB. The at-home spouse can keep $75,000. Some people may ask why the at-home spouse cannot keep up to $92,760 instead of just the one-half share of $75,000. This is a good question, and you might lobby your elected state officials because some states do combine the minimum and maximum amounts.

Example 3: The total countable resources of a couple are $280,000. The CSRA equals the *greater* of the **state** minimum resource allowance ($31,290) or one-half of the couple's total countable resources (here $140,000) up to $92,760. Under this rule the at-home spouse may keep $92,760. The remaining resources (other than excluded resources) owned by the couple must be spent on the ill spouse's care until the ill spouse qualifies for NHB. Some people think it is unfair that the couple in Example 2 may only

---

[19]In 1995 HSD started to allow the at-home spouse to spend down the ill spouse's share of resources on excluded property, such as paying off a mortgage or buying a home or car, or purchasing an immediate annuity for the life of the at-home spouse.

keep $75,000, but the more wealthy couple in this example gets to keep $92,760.

According to HSD no matter how many resources a couple owns, if the at-home spouse has resources worth more than the **federal** maximum standard, $92,760 for 2004, then the ill spouse will not be eligible for NHB until the ill spouse has spent down his or her share to the amounts discussed in the beginning of this chapter and the at-home (community) spouse has spent down his or her share to $92,760 or less. Of course, the ill spouse is free to transfer resources to the children or others, subject to the penalty periods discussed previously. During the transfer penalty period, the couple would be responsible for paying the full cost of nursing home care for the ill spouse.

In all of the above examples it is important to know that after HSD decides that the ill spouse is eligible for NHB, resources equal to the amount of the CSRA may be transferred to the at-home spouse. HSD regulations advise that the transfers take place as soon as possible, but all transfers must be completed **within 12 months from the date of the initial assessment.**

Home Not a Countable Resource

The best news for married couples regards the home. State and federal regulations provide that as long as the at-home spouse remains in the community (i.e., is not also institutionalized) at any time prior to or after the other spouse's institutionalization, the homestead may be transferred to the at-home (community) spouse.[20] If the home is **transferred** to the community spouse in his or her name only, the community spouse does not actually have

---

[20]If the ill spouse is mentally incapacitated, then the community spouse must have a valid durable power of attorney that authorizes such a transfer. The power of attorney must have been signed by the ill spouse before becoming incapacitated. If no such power of attorney exists, a conservator must be appointed in order for the community spouse to transfer the home to himself or herself. Chapter One discusses powers of attorney and conservatorships in detail.

to reside in the home. If the deed to the home has both spouses' names on it, then the community spouse must actually reside in the home in order for the home to be excluded.

After the ill spouse is receiving NHB, if the at-home spouse sells the homestead that is now in the at-home spouse's sole name, the at-home spouse can keep the entire proceeds from the sale without contributing any portion to the ill spouse. As discussed above, however, the ill spouse may be penalized if the at-home spouse then transferred all or some of the sale proceeds to third parties or sold the home for less than fair market value.

Separate Resources of Spouse at Risk

Normally under community property principles, resources belonging to one party **before the marriage** are the **separate** property of that individual. In the NHB program, however, after HSD determines that an applicant's income is within the eligibility limits, federal law mandates that community property laws no longer apply. In essence, federal law overrides (preempts) state community property law. This means HSD must follow certain federal regulations in calculating a couple's resources.

For purposes of NHB **all** of a couple's resources, separate and community, are added together to calculate the amount of their resources. The total amount of resources, both separate and community, is divided by two. This method of calculating may impose an unfair result for couples in second marriages or where one spouse owns considerably more resources than the other.

Many couples marry for a second time late in life. For example, Wife may bring her separate resources worth $200,000 to the marriage. **New Mexico** community property law states that Wife's $200,000 is her separate property. She may have a will that leaves the resources to her children from her first marriage rather than to her new husband. Husband may bring his separate resources of $50,000 to the marriage. Assume that Husband requires nursing home care and meets the NHB program income requirements. Under **federal** law HSD will look at the resources of both Husband and Wife and divide by two. Remember the CSRA equals the *greater* of the **state** minimum resource allowance ($31,290) or one-half of the couple's total countable resources up to $92,760, in this example $125,000. Under this rule Wife can keep only $92,760 of the couple's total resources. The remaining countable resources owned by the couple, **including Wife's separate resources**, must be spent on Husband's care until he qualifies for NHB.

Couples can protect themselves from this result in several ways. If an at-home spouse is forced to spend his or her separate resources on the ill spouse's care, the at-home spouse may seek a court order that will protect his or her separate property. Some couples seek a court-ordered division of property or divorce (discussed in more detail beginning on page 86), during which the court distributes the couple's separate property to each of them. The at-home spouse may be awarded all of his or her separate resources and HSD will be unable to force the resources to be spent on the ill spouse's care. This is a harsh method of protecting property but may be necessary in some cases.

Changes in Circumstances of Ill or At-Home Spouse

New Mexico's regulations require that changes in income be reported to the HSD caseworker **within ten days** of the change. HSD will then reconsider the eligibility of the ill spouse for NHB. Other changes should also be reported to HSD, such as the death or institutionalization of the at-home spouse, the death of the ill spouse or the recovery of the ill spouse so that the ill spouse no longer requires nursing home care.

Death of At-Home Spouse

Sometimes even though the ill spouse requires nursing home care, the at-home spouse will die before the ill spouse dies. If the at-home spouse dies and the will leaves all of the resources to the ill spouse, these resources will make the ill spouse ineligible for NHB. The inherited resources will have to be spent down until the ill spouse is again eligible for NHB. The at-home spouse can avoid this result by updating the will to disinherit the ill (institutionalized) spouse and leaving resources to children or other beneficiaries. Designating a beneficiary other than the ill spouse on life insurance policies, IRAs and other accounts may be wise. New Mexico's laws on wills contain certain protections for spouses (see Chapter Four on wills and family and personal property allowances). Also IRA and annuity provisions may limit who can be a beneficiary. Estate tax consequences of omitting a spouse from one's will should also be analyzed. The at-home spouse should consult an attorney familiar with this area of the law to make sure that the resources are best protected.

What If You Disagree with HSD?

If an applicant disagrees with HSD about aspects of the NHB program eligibility, such as income, resources or trusts, the applicant can ask for an administrative fair hearing before HSD. An administrative law judge will hear evidence from the applicant and from HSD and will decide if the applicant was wrongfully denied benefits. If either spouse is not satisfied with a CSRA or CSMIA determination, HSD regulations also provide for an administrative fair hearing. If a fair hearing decision is unfavorable to the applicant, the applicant may file an appeal with the New Mexico Court of Appeals. People who are initially denied benefits often challenge HSD successfully at the fair hearing level. Those who are not satisfied with the result of the fair hearing often challenge a decision successfully at the court of appeals.

Problems with Medicaid (Nursing Home Benefits Program) Benefits

- ❑ The individual who receives Medicaid is allowed to have very few resources.
- ❑ Medicaid does not pay for everything, such as a private room or unlimited hearing aids.

❑ Some nursing homes may provide nicer facilities for non-Medicaid (private pay) patients. This may be illegal, but hard to prove.

❑ Some nursing homes may discriminate against admitting Medicaid patients. This is illegal, but hard to prove.

❑ Number of Medicaid beds in a particular facility may be limited.

❑ Medicaid only pays for intermediate or skilled nursing home care and not for shelter care homes, home health care or boarding homes, except on a limited basis.

Ways to Protect Your Resources

Many people have strong feelings about whether they should spend all of their resources on their own care or attempt to preserve some of their resources to pass on to their children or other beneficiaries. To pay for nursing home care, some people will attempt to transfer large amounts of resources in order to become eligible for Medicaid. They believe they have worked hard to save money and they would like to pass on their property to their children, not to the nursing home.

Others feel that they have earned their money for their own use and they want to spend their money on their care. These people do not believe that children have an automatic right to inherit their money, especially if the taxpayers (whose taxes pay for the Medicaid program) pay for their care. They prefer to pay their own way as long as they can. This book will not attempt to discuss the ethics of either position. The analysis depends on the financial position of the individual, the individual's marital status and the financial positions of the children, as well as other considerations. The choice is quite personal and must be decided by each individual.

Some people may simply be ineligible for NHB due to high monthly income or other reasons. They need to plan ahead in case they require nursing home care in the future. For those who wish to preserve as many resources as they can for an at-home spouse or for future beneficiaries, there are several ways to do so.

Convert countable resources to non-countable resources. Certain resources are not counted when determining a person's eligibility for NHB. Between spouses, the home, car and furnishings are not counted. One way to preserve some of a couple's resources is to convert countable resources (like cash, stocks, bonds, etc.) to non-countable resources. This might include making major home repairs or additions, paying off a home mortgage, buying a new car or purchasing a new refrigerator or furnace **prior to or after** the time a spouse enters a nursing home or is institutionalized for more than 30 days. Depending on the couple's total assets, it might be wise to wait until the ill spouse is institutionalized in order to maximize the amount the at-home spouse can keep. Buying numerous Picasso prints or expensive Southwestern pots is not recommended, as HSD will probably consider these items investments rather than personal items or household furnishings.

Single individuals will find it more difficult to convert countable resources to non-countable resources. Buying a burial space and a prepaid irrevocable insurance policy payable to the funeral home is about the only choice.

Buy long-term-care insurance. In recent years insurance companies have created insurance policies that pay for nursing home or other long-term care. Premiums for these policies can run $100 a month or more, but the premiums may be deductible as medical expenses on Schedule A of a person's income tax return. If the policy pays off as promised, buying such insurance can be worthwhile. The New Mexico Legislature passed the Long-Term Care Insurance Act, which regulates insurance companies that offer long-term-care insurance. Some questions to ask before buying a long-term-care insurance policy include:

❑ How long has the company offered this policy?
❑ How long has the company been in business?

❑ What is the monthly premium for this policy? Must the premium still be paid if the insured person requires nursing home care or other care, or is the premium waived?

❑ Is the premium charged guaranteed not to change for the individual policy holder unless all New Mexico policy holders are subject to a rate increase? You do not want to be penalized with a higher premium if you become ill.

❑ How much per day does the policy pay for long-term care? Does this amount increase with inflation?

❑ How long will this policy pay benefits? Look for a policy that pays for four or more years of nursing home care.

❑ What choice of waiting periods does this policy provide? Different policies have different waiting periods during which you must pay for the cost of care. The policy should cost less if you agree to pay for more days of care before the insurance company starts paying.

❑ Will the policy pay for a case management/care coordinator to help plan your care?

❑ Is the policy a tax-qualified plan for income tax purposes?

❑ For spouses, does the policy provide a survivorship benefit right or option to provide all levels of care to the surviving spouse?

❑ Is the policy guaranteed renewable regardless of age or health?

❑ What kinds of coverage does the policy provide? Skilled nursing care? Intermediate care? Custodial care at a shelter care home or boarding home? Will the policy pay for care in the patient's home? The more kinds of coverage offered, the better the policy.

❑ Does the policy require hospitalization immediately prior to nursing home care? (New Mexico law contains certain restrictions against this.)

Give it all away. Some people prefer to give away all or some of their resources in order to become eligible for Medicaid. Ideally transfers should be made more than 36 months before the transferor requires nursing home care. Those who transfer their resources might ask the recipients to keep the resources for them in case of an emergency or with other restrictions. However, after the resources are transferred, the recipient has no **legal** obligation to preserve the resources. Depending on the amount of the resources transferred, the individual will be ineligible for NHB until the expiration of the transfer penalty period discussed earlier.

Create certain trusts. Prior to August 11, 1993, certain irrevocable Medicaid trusts could be created to shelter the resources of an applicant seeking NHB. The Omnibus Budget Reconciliation Act of 1993 (OBRA) now prevents many trust beneficiaries from becoming eligible for NHB. Irrevocable Medicaid trusts can no longer be used to shelter an applicant's resources, although such trusts created before August 11 may still be valid. Keep in mind that trusts established by a **third party** through a will, trust or separate document using the resources of the third party are not subject to these OBRA limitations. Several other exceptions also exist:

Income Diversion Trusts: This trust allows certain individuals whose *resources* (discussed beginning on page 60) meet HSD guidelines, but whose *income* exceeds the $1,692 limit (for 2004), to put a portion of the income into an income diversion trust. The trustee (manager of the trust) can only pay out of the trust an amount of money that allows the individual to become eligible for NHB benefits. The trust limits the trustee's power to distributing funds each month to an amount which, when combined with other income, is $1.00 below the Medicaid income cap. When the individual dies, the money remaining in the trust goes to the state Human Services Department up to the amount of NHB paid by HSD on behalf of the individual.

Income diversion trusts are allowed for both single and married individuals. The trust will help those who have spent down most of their resources or who have very few resources, but whose income is over the Medicaid income cap. The Senior Citizens Law Office in Albuquerque, 265-2300, can provide more information on these trusts.

Trusts for Disabled: A parent, grandparent, legal guardian or a court may create a trust for an individual who is under age 65 and "disabled" as defined under federal law, thus allowing the individual to receive NHB. Funds remaining in the trust at the individual's death must be paid to the state up to an amount equal to the benefits paid on behalf of the applicant.

Pooled Trusts for Disabled: A nonprofit association may manage a pooled trust for a disabled individual of any age. Separate accounts for each individual must be kept. These trusts may be established by the disabled individual, as well as the individual's parent, grandparent, legal guardian or a court. The amounts not retained in the pool at the individual's death must be paid to the state up to an amount equal to the benefits paid on behalf of the applicant.

Except for income diversion trusts, all of the above trusts, including trusts created by third parties, established to allow trust beneficiaries to remain on Medicaid, must contain "special needs" or "supplemental needs" provisions. These provisions allow the trustee to pay for items not covered by NHB or other benefits programs. The trustee (manager) of the trust must follow strict guidelines in distributing trust assets and is not allowed to spend trust monies if doing so would make the beneficiary ineligible for NHB or other benefits. The rules governing the distribution of funds and the reporting requirements are complicated. Whoever serves as trustee must be aware of all the requirements in order to keep the trust beneficiary eligible for benefits.

Obtain a court-ordered division of property or divorce. Spending down half of a couple's resources in order to become eligible for NHB may produce extremely unfair results, especially in cases of second marriages where the at-home spouse owns most of the resources as separate property and does not want to spend half of the resources on the ill spouse's care or if spending half of a couple's resources would drastically alter the lifestyle of the at-home spouse. A court-ordered division of property or divorce might also be appropriate for a couple whose joint income is too high for one spouse to qualify for NHB.

In these cases the at-home spouse can hire an attorney to go to court and seek a court-ordered division of property or divorce. If the ill spouse is mentally incompetent, the court will appoint a *guardian ad litem* (attorney) to represent the ill spouse's best interests. As part of the court-ordered division of property or divorce, the judge will order that the couple's property be divided in a certain way. The judge will consider the circumstances of both parties and may divide the property in such a way that the ill spouse is eligible for NHB. Court-ordered divisions of property and divorce may now be more difficult to use. HSD has begun closely examining these proceedings and may try to ignore proceedings that unfairly divide property.

Seeking a court-ordered division of property or divorce, especially in cases where couples have been married for many years, can be emotionally stressful. The couple and the family must consider the financial advantages, the emotional disadvantages, the tax consequences and the affect on benefits and other resources that a court-ordered division of property or divorce would create.

Estate Recovery Law Now Federally Mandated

OBRA 1993 requires every state to enact an estate recovery law that allows each state to recover certain benefits paid on behalf of an individual for services rendered after the recipient reaches age 55. If a person has spent down all of his or her resources, obviously the state could not recover anything. But in some instances, for example the Coordinated Community In-Home Care (CCIC) program, individuals are allowed to remain in their home and to receive CCIC benefits (see also footnote, page 56).

Under the estate recovery law, after the recipient of benefits dies, the state could recover monies paid on behalf of the individual who received benefits by selling the home or liquidating other assets. The state cannot make any recoveries while a spouse or minor, blind or disabled child is still living. Certain undue hardship exceptions also exist.

Some states have passed laws allowing the state to place liens on the real property (houses, land, etc.) of individuals receiving NHB and, upon the death of the person receiving the benefits, to sell the property and recover monies up to the amount spent on the individual's care. In 1994 New Mexico passed an estate recovery act that allows recovery for benefits paid for nursing facilities, home and community-based services, and related hospital and prescription drug services, but does **not** include lien provisions. New Mexico's law allows recovery only from **probate** estate assets, discussed in Chapter Six. Contact your local HSD office for details.

This area of the law is complex and confusing. More attorneys are becoming knowledgeable about spousal-impoverishment provisions and NHB. HSD employees should be able to answer questions about transferring resources and income/resource eligibility requirements for NHB. Planning ahead can help preserve some or all of a couple's resources, depending on the size of the estate. The following summarizes the basic information to consider when anticipating that one spouse will require nursing home care:

1. Will your resources generate enough income to pay for nursing home care, starting at around $3,500 a month?
2. If not, is your total monthly income $1,692 or less? If income is less than $1,692, go to 3. If income is more than $1,692 and you are married, add both spouses' total monthly income and divide by two to determine each one's income.
3. If income meets eligibility requirements, consider applying for NHB. The NHB program spends Medicaid dollars to

provide nursing home care for individuals. Eligibility for NHB is based on the applicant's **income** and **resources**.

4. How much and what type resources do you have? Remember after the ill spouse is determined eligible for NHB, New Mexico's community property principles do not apply. No matter who owns the resources, half of them must be spent down, either on the ill spouse's care or on exempt assets for the at-home spouse (down to the $92,760 limit).

5. If you wish to transfer your resources to children or other third parties, try to do so **36 months or more** before entering the nursing home.

6. If transfers are not made 36 months before entering the nursing home, a penalty period probably applies.

7. No penalties are assessed on transfers between spouses. However, the at-home spouse is only allowed to keep a certain amount of resources, the **greater of $31,290 or one-half of the couple's resources up to $92,760**.

8. Certain resources are not counted, such as the home, car and personal property.

9. Convert countable resources to non-countable resources, either before or after the ill spouse enters the nursing home or is institutionalized for 30 days, depending on the couple's total assets.

10. The at-home spouse can keep income from $1,515 to $2,319/month, or more, under certain circumstances.

4

NEW MEXICO LAW REGARDING WILLS

Many people have questions about wills. If a person dies without a will, does the state get everything? What if all of the property is in joint tenancy? Can a person protect some assets for children from a first marriage? Is a handwritten will valid? Is a will from another state valid in New Mexico? How can a person ensure that a new spouse will not get all of the assets? If a person has a will, does that mean there will be no probate?

A **will**[1] is a legal document that gives instructions to a **personal representative** about how to distribute assets to the **beneficiaries**. Beneficiaries named in a will are called **devisees** by New Mexico law, although many people refer to the beneficiaries as **heirs**. If a person dies without a will, the beneficiaries are called **heirs** by New Mexico law.[2] The person making the will is called the **testator**. In a will you name the personal representative (other states' laws may call this person an executor or administrator) to carry out the terms of your will. You then name the people you want to receive your assets. A will may also name a guardian for minor or disabled children.

---

[1] New Mexico's law on wills appears in the New Mexico Statutes Annotated, Sections 45-2-101 through 45-2-902. These statutes are available at the University of New Mexico School of Law Library (Albuquerque), the New Mexico Supreme Court Library (Santa Fe), the New Mexico State University Library located in Branson Hall (Las Cruces) and at various attorneys' offices. You may also purchase copies of these statutes directly from the New Mexico Compilation Commission, PO Box 15549, Santa Fe NM 87506; (505) 827-4821.

[2] This book may also use the term "heirs" as a generic word referring to beneficiaries of an estate. Technically, heirs are those who inherit an estate when there is no will.

Why Have a Will?
- ❏ Peace of mind.
- ❏ Exercising control over how your property is distributed.
- ❏ Choosing your personal representative.
- ❏ You may think you do not need a will because all of your assets are held in joint accounts, joint tenancy or through beneficiary accounts. However, you might acquire separate assets through inheritance, gift or by winning a lottery (probably a long shot). Remember that even if you hold assets in joint tenancy, if the other joint tenant dies, you are then the sole owner of the assets.
- ❏ You own separate property (in your name only) or property in another county or state.
- ❏ You wish to leave your property to people other than your spouse or children, such as friends, charity or others.
- ❏ You need to make arrangements for the care of a disabled adult or minor child.
- ❏ You wish to appoint a guardian for a minor child or establish a trust for children or grandchildren.
- ❏ You wish to give certain items of personal property to certain people or to designate the distribution of items of tangible personal property though a supplemental list.

New Mexico Law on Wills

New Mexico law allows "an individual eighteen or more years of age who is of sound mind" to make a will. People "of sound mind" should know what a will does, what kind of property they own and who they want to inherit their assets. A person with an eccentric personality or habits may be "of sound mind" for purposes of making a will. But if an individual is confused, suffering from dementia and/or unable to understand what a will does, the individual is probably not "of sound mind" for purposes of making a will. A New Mexico case, however, does allow an individual during a "lucid moment" to sign a will if, at the time of signing, the individual understood what he or she was doing.

Contents of a Will

Wills vary depending on who prepares them. Common provisions of a will include:

- ❑ Statement that this is your will and it revokes all prior wills.
- ❑ Statement of family history, listing spouses and children by name.
- ❑ Appointment of a personal representative and an alternate personal representative.
- ❑ Summary of the personal representative's duties and powers.
- ❑ Directions on how your debts will be paid.
- ❑ Instructions about family and personal property allowances (if you are married or have minor or dependent children).
- ❑ Specific gifts to people, such as "I devise $100 to my friend Ann Jimenez." Often a will also states what happens if Ann Jimenez dies before you, such as whether the gift lapses and becomes part of the residuary of your estate or whether the gift passes on to Ann Jimenez's children or others. Your will should state clearly what happens to Ann Jimenez's gift if she dies before you.
- ❑ Reference to a list of tangible personal property (discussed in more detail on page 110).
- ❑ Residuary clause, i.e., who gets the bulk of your estate. Also, what happens to each gift if one of your beneficiaries dies before you die (you basically choose alternate people to receive the gift; then if your beneficiaries die, you do not have to change your will each time). The residuary clause often says, "I leave my property to X, *per stirpes*." *Per stirpes* means that if X has died, **X's share** of your estate is divided in equal parts among X's children. If X has no children, X's share will probably be divided among the

other named beneficiaries. The terms *per capita* or "share and share alike" may also appear in a will. *Per capita* means that all of the named beneficiaries receive an equal share of the estate. If the will states, "I leave my property to X, Y and Z, *per capita*," X, Y and Z will each receive one-third of the estate. If X has died, then Y and Z will each receive one-half of the estate.

❑ A clause, usually called the *"in terrorem"* clause, that dissuades people from challenging the terms of your will.

❑ Signature and date lines for you and two witnesses.

❑ Self-proving clause with signature lines for you and two witnesses and a place for the notary public to sign and stamp or seal the will.

Your will passes all property that is **in your name only** to your beneficiaries. A court proceeding is usually required to carry out the terms of a will. This court proceeding is called a **probate**, discussed in Chapter Six. However, if your assets are worth $30,000 or less and are not real estate, your beneficiaries may be able to sign an **affidavit of successor in interest,** also discussed in Chapter Six, and avoid a probate. If your assets include any real estate (land, houses, oil and gas rights) or personal property worth over $30,000 that is not held in joint tenancy or in some other arrangement (such an insurance policy that names a beneficiary or a "payable on death" bank account), a probate will be necessary. **Having a will does not get you out of a probate!** The will does, however, state your wishes about who inherits and who will serve as your personal representative.

Choosing a Personal Representative

As defined above, the **personal representative** ((called an executor or administrator in other states) is the person named in a will to carry out the terms of the will (Chapter Six on probate includes more discussion on the responsibilities and tasks of a personal representative). After you die, your personal representative handles your business matters and distributes your assets. The more you tell your personal representative before you die, the better your personal representative will be able to act for your estate.

Before choosing a personal representative, it is wise to discuss the responsibilities the personal representative is agreeing to undertake. Your personal representative should be familiar with your assets, where you keep records and where your original will is stored. Some of my clients have created a panic book that contains some or all of the following:

❑ Burial instructions, including cemetery location, whether you have a prepaid plot or burial insurance, whether you wish to be cremated, whether you have donated your body for medical research, whether you are an organ donor, etc.

❑ Location of your most recent will (many people give the personal representative a copy of the will).

❑ Lists of relatives and other beneficiaries with current addresses and phone numbers.

❑ If you have minor children, instructions about whom you have named in your will as guardian and whether you have made special financial arrangements for the children through life insurance or other means.

❑ Lists of others to be notified if you die (doctors, accountants, Social Security Administration, friends, Motor Vehicle Division, insurance companies, etc.).

❑ Information on whether you have a safe deposit box (or boxes), including where you keep the key; some people include a list of the contents of the safe deposit box.

❑ Lists of assets, including bank accounts, stocks, bonds, real property (houses, ranches and other land), other investments, account numbers, in whose name the accounts are listed, brokers' names and phone numbers. Include a **date** on this list so your personal representative knows how current the list is; **update this list as your assets change**. If you do not make a list, your personal representative will have to figure out what assets you have based on what statements arrive in the mail over a period of time and your income tax return.

❑ List of important papers such as Social Security card; Medicare card; military discharge papers; deeds to real estate; titles to mobile homes or motor vehicles; birth, marriage, divorce or other legal papers.

❑ List of all insurance policies, including homeowner, accident, life, auto, etc. Include the company name, policy number, named beneficiary and location of the actual policy.

❑ Information on IRAs, pensions, profit-sharing plans with the name of the company, account number and name of the beneficiary.

❑ Tax records, including recent federal and state income tax and property tax information, where returns are stored and whether you have an accountant.

❑ Information about personal effects.

❑ List of credit cards and charge accounts, with account numbers and location of the cards.

❑ Whether you have a home safe or other strongbox; if so, make sure someone you trust has the combination and/or knows where the keys are.

❑ Any other information you may want to pass on (how to access the genealogical records in your computer, family memories, whom you would like to care for your pet, etc.).

Gathering all of this information will probably seem cumbersome. But having the information in one place will prove invaluable to anyone who, due to your incapacity or death, assists with your financial affairs. Sometimes people throw out a deceased person's papers too soon. The personal representative should keep all of the papers belonging to the deceased person until all business matters have been resolved.

Your personal representative does **not** have to be a New Mexico resident. You may also choose to appoint co-personal representatives, but your will should specify when both of their signatures are required and how to resolve any differences.

Choosing Beneficiaries

If you are **single**, you may leave your assets to **whomever you wish**, as long as you do not have minor children or children with special needs who depend on you for support. You have **no legal duty** to leave your assets to your adult children, although many people do.

Many parents leave their assets to their children. Other parents do not get along with their children, or the children are wealthy and do not need the assets. People may instead select grandchildren or other relatives, friends, a church, synagogue, educational institution, or favorite charity as recipients. You must create a valid will or trust that clearly states your intent.

If your will cuts out your children, they may try to contest the will in court. They will probably lose if the will is valid, if the will names the children and states that you specifically intended to omit them, and if you were "of sound mind" when you made the will.

If you are **married**, a portion of the community property (*see* page 58) already belongs to the surviving spouse, unless a prenuptial agreement or trust specifies otherwise. You can leave your portion of the community property to whomever you wish.

Other people leave bequests to universities for scholarships or other uses. The language in your will should specify the name and address of the university or school, the name of the scholarship, what department or school the scholarship is for (such as nursing, engineering, education, arts and sciences, medical school) and the criteria to be used to choose recipients of the scholarship monies (such as academic standards, financial need or other criteria).

Your will or trust should clearly identify the charities you wish to benefit, including names and complete addresses. You might also contact the charity beforehand and ask if it would like other information included in the bequest. You should state what happens if that particular charity no longer exists at your death, perhaps designating an alternate charity or recipient.

Some people may make bequests to universities for scholarships or other uses. To create a scholarship earmarked for a particular purpose, the language in your will or trust should specify the name and address of the university or school, the name of the scholarship, what department or school the scholarship is for (such as nursing, engineering, education, arts and sciences, medical school) and the criteria that should be used to choose recipients of the scholarship monies (such as academic standards, financial need, or other criteria).

If your will or trust omits your children, the children could try to contest the document in court. Be sure to choose a knowledgeable attorney to draft your will or trust. Your will or trust should withstand a court challenge if:

❑ the document includes language that names the children and states that you specifically intend to omit them;

❑ you were "of sound mind" when you made the document;

❑ you created the document "of your own free will;" and,

❑ the document was properly executed.

Adopted Children's Rights

According to New Mexico law, "An adopted individual is the child of his adopting parent or parents and not of his natural parents...." Most state laws treat adopted children as blood relatives of their adopting parents and as strangers to their natural parents.

New Mexico's law is different if a child is adopted by the new spouse of the child's natural parent. "The adoption of a child by the spouse of either natural parent has no effect on ... the right of the child or a descendant of the child to inherit from or through the other natural parent," states New Mexico law.

Suppose Ruslyn is the natural child of Bert and Julia, who divorce. Julia marries Mark, who adopts Ruslyn. If all of the parents involved died without a valid will, under New Mexico law, Ruslyn could inherit from Julia and Mark, as well as from Bert.

If Bert does not want this to happen, he should prepare a will that states his intention to disinherit Ruslyn. This example of stepparent adoption is the one exception to the general rule that adopted children lose their inheritance rights from their blood parents.

Does a natural parent have a financial obligation to a child who was adopted by strangers many years ago? No. If the natural parent wants to include that child as a beneficiary of an estate (and one has no legal or moral obligation to do so), the natural parent would need to make a will that states the wishes to include the child as a beneficiary.

More on *Per Stirpes* and By Representation

One may encounter the terms *per stirpes* (the share of each deceased child is divided among his/her surviving descendants) or **by representation** (the shares of deceased descendants are pooled and divided into equal shares based on number of surviving descendants of deceased descendants on that level). By representation is the concept used in New Mexico for an intestate estate, but *per stirpes* often appears in wills.

Per Stirpes/By Representation Example: Bob died, leaving an estate of $300,000. He had no surviving spouse. Bob had three children, two of whom are deceased. Child 1 is living and has 2 children; Child 2 had three children; Child 3 had one child.

Under either concept, Child 1 inherits $100,000. Child 1's children inherit nothing because Child 1 is still alive.

Under *per stirpes*, Child 2's three children would split Child 2's $100,000, each receiving $33,333.33. Child 3's child would receive Child 3's entire share of $100,000.

Under by representation, the shares of Child 2 and Child 3 ($200,000) would be added together and then split equally among their four children, each receiving $50,000.

Omitting Spouse and Children from Will

New Mexico law contains specific provisions about omitting a spouse or child from a will.

If a testator's surviving spouse married the testator after the will was made, "the surviving spouse is entitled to receive, as an intestate share (discussed on page 121), no less than the value of the share of the estate he would have received if the testator had died intestate" to the extent that the share is not devised to a child born before the marriage and who is not a child of the surviving spouse, unless it appears that the will:

(1) was made in contemplation of the subsequent marriage,

(2) expresses the intent that it is to be effective notwithstanding any subsequent marriage, or

(3) the testator provided for the spouse by transfer outside the will.

Your intent to provide for the spouse outside of the will must be clear, such as transferring funds to joint bank accounts or changing the beneficiary on a retirement plan to the spouse.

If you do not update your will after remarrying, the above provision means your children from a prior marriage receive your property. If you wish to include a new spouse in your will, be sure and make a new will after remarrying.

The law is silent about omitting children born **before** the will is made, but contains provisions about omitting children born **after** a will is made.

If you **intend** to omit a child born **before** you made your will, state law no longer requires you to mention the child in your will. Most attorneys recommend making any omission very clear in your will or trust. Do not be too detailed; a simple statement such as, "I specifically intend to omit my children A, B and C as beneficiaries of this will (or trust)" should be sufficient.

The **omitted children** provisions state that if you fail to provide for children born or adopted **after** you sign your will, the children may be entitled to a certain portion of your estate unless you make it clear in your will that you **intend** to omit them. You may also provide for an omitted after-born or after-adopted child by transferring property to the child outside of the will.

Name on Account/Property Determines Ownership

The most important piece of information in this book is: **property that has *any name* other than your name (whether as a joint tenant, payable on death beneficiary, transfer on death, or other named beneficiary) will *not* be affected by or pass through your will!** Property held as **tenants in common** (see Example 6 on page 106) is subject to different rules.

Joint tenancy property is not affected by a will. Many deeds to houses or other real property contain the words "joint tenants." This means that the individuals who own the property each own an equal share of the property. Upon the death of one joint tenant, the surviving joint tenant **automatically** owns the entire property, no matter what the will says.

Bank accounts, stock accounts and other accounts can also be joint tenancy accounts. The title to bank or stock accounts may read (1) "X or Y as joint tenants," (2) "X and Y as joint tenants," (3) "X and Y as joint tenants with right of survivorship," (4) "X or Y," or (5) "X and Y." When a bank account is an "or" account, **either** X or Y can sign checks or withdraw the entire amount of the account. When a bank account is an "and" account, **both** X and Y must sign checks or withdrawal slips. Upon the death of X or Y, the survivor owns the entire account.

Parents will often add the name of a child to a bank account as a joint tenant. The parents may not realize that the child can then withdraw all of the assets from the account without the parents' permission. Also, if the child is sued or goes bankrupt, the parents' account can be attached to pay the debts of the child. The parents' account can also be attached to pay state and federal tax liens against the child if the child's name is on the parents' bank account. While joint tenancy accounts avoid probate, individuals should also recognize the drawbacks of joint tenancy accounts.

People who add the name of another to an account often do so in case they become incapacitated. Signing a power of attorney would also allow someone to access accounts *without* having ownership interests in the accounts.

Payable on Death accounts are not affected by a will. New Mexico law allows individuals who have bank, credit union, and savings and loan accounts, such as checking, savings and certificates of deposit, to set up a "payable on death" (POD) account. POD accounts pass automatically to the named beneficiary. POD accounts are simple to set up. The owner of the account simply signs a card at the bank, credit union, or savings and loan office that designates the account as POD and lists the POD beneficiaries.

For example, the name on the account will read, "Saul Jones, POD in equal shares to Amy Jones, Wendell Jones and Kris Jones." This means that the account is Saul Jones's own account during his lifetime. Saul's children and the children's creditors have no right to access the account during Saul's lifetime. When Saul dies, the children take his death certificate to the bank, and the bank distributes the assets in the account in equal shares to the three children. U.S. savings bonds may also have a POD beneficiary named on the bonds. Stocks and regular corporate bonds **cannot** currently be designated as POD accounts. POD accounts are a good way to pass bank accounts and U.S. savings bonds to beneficiaries without going through a probate proceeding.

Transfer on Death accounts are not affected by a will. The New Mexico legislature passed a law in 1992 that allows investment securities (stocks, bonds, mutual funds, brokerage accounts, etc.) to be titled **Transfer on Death (TOD)**. TOD accounts, similar to POD accounts, pass automatically to the named TOD beneficiary and **are not affected by a will**. For example, the name on a stock certificate may read "Ann Chavez, TOD in equal shares to Betty Chavez and John Smith." If Ann Chavez dies, her shares of stock will pass in equal shares directly to Betty Chavez and John Smith. Even if Ann Chavez's will states otherwise, the shares of stock will pass according to the TOD designation.

TOD accounts are yet another way to avoid probating certain assets. Contact your local stockbroker or investment manager and ask about TOD accounts. Brokerages are **not** required to offer TOD accounts, but the more people who ask for them, the more likely it is the brokerages will want to participate.

Beneficiary accounts are not affected by a will. Life insurance, Individual Retirement Accounts (IRA), annuities and certain pension plans all allow the owner of the policy or plan to name a beneficiary. The beneficiary automatically receives the proceeds of the insurance, IRA, annuity or pension when the owner dies. Changing a beneficiary is easy. Each company has a form for the owner to fill out that names the beneficiary. Naming an **alternate** beneficiary is wise in case the beneficiary dies before the owner. When the owner dies, the beneficiary presents the owner's death certificate to the company or plan administrator. The company or plan administrator may also have additional forms for the beneficiary to fill out. Proceeds of these accounts pass automatically to the named beneficiaries without going through a probate proceeding.

Real property with a valid "transfer on death" deed is not affected by a will. Effective July 1, 2001, a state law allows owners of real property located in New Mexico to record a "transfer on death deed" (TODD)[3] naming a beneficiary (or beneficiaries) to own that real property after the owner's death. Examples of real property include houses, land and ranches. With a properly recorded deed, no court probate is needed to transfer the real property.

The law strictly requires that, during the owner's lifetime, the TODD must be recorded with the County Clerk in the county

---

[3]New Mexico's law on transfer on death deeds appears in the New Mexico Statutes Annotated, Section 45-6-401. A sample Transfer on Death Deed form appears as part of the TODD statute.

where the real property is located. **If the deed is not properly recorded during the owner's lifetime, it is ineffective.**

Unlike a joint tenancy, where an owner transfers real property to a co-owner during his/her lifetime, the TODD is not effective until the owner dies. That means the beneficiary named in the TODD cannot control the property until after the owner dies. Nor can the beneficiary's creditors reach the property during the owner's lifetime.

The owner can revoke a TODD by recording a new TODD, or by recording a revocation in the county where the property is located. The deed is also revoked if the owner sells all of his/her interest in the real property.

A will does not affect TODDs. The TODD, not the will, controls who owns the real property after the owner's death.

However, be aware that if estate assets are insufficient to pay a decedent's debts, the beneficiary of the TODD property may be forced by creditors to use the property to pay the debts. This rule also applies to payment of the family and personal property allowances discussed later in this chapter.

TODDs require skillful drafting. Hiring a knowledgeable attorney to create a TODD is recommended.

Assets in one name only pass through a will. Assets held in only one name will probably pass to a person's beneficiaries through a probate proceeding. There are many, many ways to thwart your intentions to pass your property in equal shares to certain beneficiaries. Adding other names to accounts or property can avoid probate, but adding other names to accounts or property can also create problems. The following examples illustrate some of these problems:

Example 1: Husband and Wife are both alive. Their home is held in joint tenancy with right of survivorship, which means that if Wife dies, Husband *automatically* owns the house without any court proceeding. If Husband dies, Wife *automatically* owns the house without any court proceeding.

Example 2: Same as Example 1, except both Husband and Wife have now died. After Husband's death, Wife left the home in her name alone. Her will leaves all of her property in equal shares to her children. The house will pass through a probate (court) proceeding to the children, according to the terms of Wife's will.

Example 3: Husband and Wife have four children, all over age eighteen. Husband and Wife's home is held in joint tenancy with right of survivorship. Husband dies. Wife adds the name of one child to the house deed, along with her own name, as joint tenant with right of survivorship. Wife signs a will that leaves everything in equal shares to the four children. Wife dies. The house will pass *automatically* to the child whose name is on the deed. The child has no legal obligation to share the house with the other three children. **The will only passes property that is in Wife's name only.** If Wife added the one child's name as a joint tenant to all of the bank accounts, car and stocks, that child would receive everything and the other three children would receive nothing. The one child might have a *moral* obligation to divide the assets equally, but not a legal obligation. If the other three children sued the one child for their shares, they would probably lose unless they could prove undue influence or fraud.

Example 4: This is a second marriage for both Husband and Wife. Each brings separate property into the marriage and keeps this property in each person's own name. Husband's will leaves everything to Wife, but if Wife dies first, then to Husband's children from his first marriage. Wife's will leaves everything to Husband, but if Husband dies first, then to Wife's children from her first marriage. Wife dies. Husband now owns everything. This was not what Wife meant to do, but it is too late. Husband's children will now get everything, unless Husband includes Wife's children from her first marriage in his will.

Example 5: Same circumstances as Example 4 except Husband and Wife designated their separate bank accounts as payable on death (POD) to their own children. Wife dies. Her children will share her bank accounts automatically without a probate proceeding. Wife's other assets that are in her name only will pass through a probate proceeding, according to the terms of her will.

Example 6: Ms. Gallegos owns her home, titled in her sole name. She creates a Transfer on Death Deed to the home, naming her daughter Mary Lou as the beneficiary. She records the deed in the county clerk's office during her lifetime. Ms. Gallegos dies. Her will says her home is to be divided equally among her four children. Who owns the home? Mary Lou. The other three children receive nothing, because a will does not affect property passing with a properly created and recorded transfer on death deed.

Example 7: Same circumstances as Example 6, except Ms. Gallegos does not record the transfer on death deed during her lifetime. Who owns the home at her death? All four children inherit the home according to her will. This is because the transfer on death deed fails due to Ms. Gallegos' failure to record it during her lifetime.

Example 8: Mark and Josie, two unmarried individuals, own a home. The deed to the home states that Mark and Josie own the home as "tenants in common," **not** as joint tenants. This means that Mark owns one-half of the property and Josie owns one-half of the property. Mark and Josie each have wills that leave everything to their own brothers and sisters. Josie dies. Josie's half of the home will pass to Josie's brothers and sisters through a probate proceeding in court. Mark will own his half of the home with Josie's brothers and sisters.

Before you add another person's name to your property, make sure you understand what effects the addition of the name will have. If you intend for one child to receive all of your property at your death and if you intend to cut out the other children, then adding one child's name to all of your property will accomplish this. But if you intend that all of your children receive equal shares of your property, adding one child's name to the property will not accomplish this goal. Remember the important rules discussed above:

❑ **Property held in joint tenancy passes automatically to the survivor and is not affected by your will.**

❑ **Property that passes to a named beneficiary passes to the beneficiary automatically and is not affected by your will.**

❑ **Property in a POD account passes automatically to the POD beneficiary and is not affected by your will.**

❑ **Property in a TOD account passes automatically to the TOD beneficiary and is not affected by your will.**

❑ **Real property with a valid TODD passes automatically to the TODD beneficiary and is not affected by your will.**

How to Create or Claim POD or TOD Property

The mechanics of creating a POD beneficiary for bank accounts and CDs or TOD beneficiary for stock securities may vary from institution to institution. But most banks, credit unions and stock brokerage firms have forms for you to name a beneficiary or beneficiaries to receive your accounts after your death. No attorney is required.

You can name one or more individuals as beneficiaries. Although not every institution requires all of this information, you should have available the beneficiary's name, address, relationship, date of birth and social security number. If applicable, you should designate the percentage of the account allotted to each beneficiary. If you are married and the beneficiary is not a spouse, spousal consent may be required.

You can also name a specific charity, school or other entity as beneficiary. Bring the entity's name, address and tax identification number.

Brokerage TOD beneficiary forms are often notarized by notaries available on site. Bank POD beneficiary forms are not usually notarized.

Some forms may allow you to name alternate beneficiaries in case one dies. If not, be sure and review your beneficiary designations periodically, especially if a beneficiary has predeceased you. You can also change, add or remove beneficiaries.

Several banks advised that if you name multiple POD beneficiaries, you should name "Beneficiary A AND Beneficiary B," rather than "Beneficiary A OR Beneficiary B." The "AND" designation means that both beneficiaries must appear to release the funds. The "OR" designation would allow all the funds to be released to the first beneficiary to appear. Another option would be to create separate CDs for each beneficiary and name only one beneficiary per CD.

The institution will keep the original beneficiary designation form on site. You might request a copy for your records.

When the owner of the account dies, the procedure to claim the account seems fairly standard. The named beneficiary (or beneficiaries) goes to the institution with the account owner's original death certificate and proof of the beneficiary's identification, such as a driver's license. If the account has two or more owners and both have died, the beneficiary should bring original death certificates for both owners.

The brokerage firms may also require the TOD beneficiary to fill out a notarized affidavit of domicile and a transfer on death affidavit. Banks do not require these documents.

After these documents are presented, the institution should release the funds. The bank should give the beneficiary a cashier's check. Early withdrawal penalties for CDs are waived when the owner dies. Even if the CD is not yet "due," it should be released without any penalty.

The brokerage firm might open an account in the beneficiary's name or transfer the beneficiary's share of account assets to the beneficiary's pre-existing account with another brokerage.

Charity as Beneficiary of Will

As discussed on page 97, one can give assets to qualified charities by will, trust or beneficiary designation.

Some people consider giving assets that are tax-deferred or have not yet been taxed, such as U.S. savings bonds, qualified retirement pensions, 401(k) and 403(b) tax-deferred plans, IRA's, annuities, payments due under an installment sale, and royalties to charities. These assets are considered **income in respect of the decedent** (IRD). Since taxes were not paid on these assets, the assets become subject to income tax, which must either be paid by the decedent's estate, the person receiving the income, or the person inheriting the right to receive the income.

Naming a charity as beneficiary of IRD income can create income tax savings. This is because qualified charities usually do not pay income tax. Therefore, the charity will receive the full benefit, for example, of a decedent's IRA. If the IRA were instead to pass to the decedent's children, the children would be responsible for paying the income tax on the IRA.

This approach might also avoid income tax if the charitable organization is identified by the decedent as the secondary IRA beneficiary, and the primary beneficiary disclaims the assets before receiving any benefit from them. Further, IRD assets can be given to charities as a specific bequest in a will or trust or as a residuary bequest if the charity is the sole residuary beneficiary.

Gifts to charity can also create estate tax savings because such gifts are deducted from the gross estate when calculating estate tax liability, discussed in Chapter Five.

Careful legal and tax planning is necessary to ensure that the donor is complying with IRS law in making gifts to charity.

Converting Joint Tenancies Upon Divorce

New Mexico law states that a divorce or annulment of a marriage "severs the interests of the former spouses in property held by them at the time of the divorce or annulment as joint tenants with the right of survivorship, transforming the interests of the former spouses into tenancies in common." A court order or contract relating to the division of marital property can override this law.

A similar law applies to decedents and killers. If you feloniously and intentionally kill someone with whom you hold property as a joint tenant, you do not inherit the whole property automatically as the surviving joint tenant (it would be bad public policy to allow such a result). Again, the interests of the decedent and killer transform into tenancies in common.

Tenancy in common means that two or more persons own an undivided interest in an asset. The interests can be equal or unequal percentages. Each tenant has the right to use and enjoy the entire property. Each tenant can will their share to whomever they want. When one tenant in common dies, that share only must be probated to pass to the heirs or devisees named in a will.

Many couples do new deeds to property when they divorce. One or the other spouse may end up with the house. However, if ex-spouses did not have a new deed prepared to their home held in joint tenancy, their interests in the home would convert to tenants in common. Each ex-spouse could then will their part of the property to their own heirs. For example, Juan and Eva marry, own their home as joint tenants, and then divorce. They do not prepare a new deed. Juan remarries Carla. Juan dies. His will leaves everything to Carla. Who owns the house now? Eva owns her half and Carla inherits Juan's half. This arrangement could prove awkward.

Divorcing couples, along with their attorneys, should sort out the titles to real property at the time of divorce to prevent future problems.

Separate List of Tangible Personal Property

Disputes about inheritances often center around an item of furniture, a photo, piece of artwork or other personal property. New Mexico law allows you to make a written statement or list of tangible personal property to give special china, silver, musical instruments, furniture, jewelry and other personal items to certain people. A will should contain language that refers to a list of **tangible** personal property only, which does **not** include other types of personal property such as stocks or bank accounts. New Mexico law is unclear as to whether you may write a separate list of tangible personal property that is not mentioned in the will. Keep any list you make with your will, so your beneficiaries will not have to search for it later.

To be valid, the list must be signed by you. The list must also describe each item and recipient "with reasonable certainty." You may **not** pass money on the list, but may pass tangible personal property, including cars, mobile homes, household items, etc. You may prepare this list before or after making your will. **You can change this list every day if you want, without having to change your will.** Just be sure to **sign** and **date** each new list you do, because your personal representative or the court will want to look at the most recent list if a dispute arises.

Also, consider who should pay to ship your tangible personal property to those who are receiving it. Should the recipient pay shipping costs or do you want your estate to pay? What if you have a piano that is going to someone across the country? The cost of shipping may be more than the piano is worth. Thinking about these issues and specifying in your will how shipping costs should be paid may prevent disputes after your death.

Personal Property and Family Allowances

New Mexico law contains two sections that reserve a certain amount of money from the estate for spouses and children of decedents who lived in New Mexico. The spouse is entitled to receive a **family allowance** of $30,000. If there is no surviving spouse, *minor and dependent* children are entitled to receive $30,000 divided by the number of minor and dependent children of the decedent. Creditors **cannot** touch this $30,000, even if debts exist. The family allowance is in addition to any inheritance that passes to the spouse and children.

New Mexico law also allows the spouse to receive from the estate of the deceased a **personal property allowance**, which is personal property valued at $15,000 or less. Personal property includes furniture, automobiles, appliances and personal effects. If there is no surviving spouse, *the decedent's children who are devisees under the will, or who are entitled to a share of the estate under omitted children provisions, or who are intestate heirs* are entitled to share the personal property allowance. Children who are specifically omitted from the will are **not** entitled to this allowance.

Again, creditors **cannot** touch this $15,000. Cash or other assets of the estate can be used to pay this allowance if personal property does not equal $15,000 in value. This personal property allowance is in addition to any inheritance that passes to the spouse and children.

If the assets in a decedent's probate estate are insufficient to pay these allowances, then the spouse or children can reach payable on death, transfer on death deed and trust property to pay them.[4]

For estates that are smaller than $45,000, the spouse or children could only receive the amount in the estate. But at least that amount would go to the survivors rather than the creditors.

A recent New Mexico case provides guidance about these allowances.[5] The *Jewell* case ruled that the surviving spouse is absolutely "entitled to [the] allowances notwithstanding contrary intentions expressed in the deceased spouse's will." The allowances must be paid before other claims are paid or distributions made.

A surviving spouse may waive the statutory allowances if certain protections are followed. To be effective, the waiver must be a written contract, agreement or waiver signed voluntarily by the surviving spouse.

---

[4]New Mexico law explicitly authorizes paying the allowances from these three types of property if probate estate assets are insufficient. The law is not so explicit about whether transfer on death property, such as stocks, bonds, and investment securities, may be used to satisfy allowances.

[5]The case citation is *In re the Estate of Jewell*, 130 N.M. 93 (Ct. App. 2001).

Trust Provisions as Part of Will

Some wills contain trust provisions. A trust within a will is called a **testamentary trust**. A testamentary trust might hold a certain amount of assets in the trust until a child reaches a certain age or might provide spending restraints for an heir who is a spendthrift. Testamentary trusts do not take effect until the death of the person who makes the trust. Chapter Five explains testamentary trusts in more detail.

Other Kinds of Wills

Holographic wills are wills in the handwriting of the testator and signed by the testator, but without proper signatures of witnesses. New Mexico does not recognize holographic wills made in this state. However, if a holographic will were validly made in a state that recognizes them, and the testator then moved here and died, the will would probably be honored here.

A **joint will** is one original will for two people. These types of wills are not favored in modern times.

Mutual wills are two identical wills for two people, usually spouses. They are also known as "I love you wills" or "mirror wills." Mutual wills leave the couple's property to each other, but if both spouses have died, then to identical successor devisees.

People may also sign wills with a contract not to revoke. Sometimes joint or mutual wills contain language that the wills cannot be revoked after the first person dies. Such a contract requires additional writings making the testator's intent clear.

Second Marriages

As mentioned in Examples 4 and 5 on page 105, second marriages can pose certain problems. Spouses should discuss what assets they have and whom they want to receive those assets after their deaths. To avoid the problem of the surviving spouse receiving all of **both** spouses' assets, spouses may set up a trust within their will. Spouses may also make arrangements through a living trust. These trusts would divide the assets of the couple into two trusts at the death of the first spouse. The assets (both separate assets brought into the marriage and community assets acquired during the marriage) of the deceased spouse would be placed into one trust. The assets (both separate assets brought into the marriage and community assets acquired during the marriage) of the surviving spouse would be placed in a second trust. A surviving spouse could use his or her own assets as he or she wished but would be limited in using the assets belonging to the deceased spouse. Chapter Five discusses trusts in more detail.

Taxable Estates and Disclaimers

Individuals whose estates total more than $1,500,000 (in 2004 and 2005) or couples whose estates total more than $3 million have taxable estates. This means that the amount of the assets over $1,500,000 (minus certain deductions) is subject to estate tax, discussed in more detail on page 148. In 2004 and 2005 estate tax rates start at 45% of the amount over $1,500,000 and rise to a maximum of 48% in 2004 and a maximum of 47% in 2005 for amounts over $2 million. A U.S. Estate Tax Return, Form 706, must be filed if an estate exceeds $1,500,000.

Federal tax laws passed in 2001 changed the amount of an estate subject to estate tax. The excluded amounts are:

2002 $1,000,000
2003 $1,000,000
2004 $1,500,000
2005 $1,500,000
2006 $2,000,000
2007 $2,000,000
2008 $2,000,000
2009 $3,500,000
2010 estate tax repealed for this year only
2011 estate tax back to 2002 number

Of course, Congress could always vote to change these amounts in the future.

Tax planning techniques exist for lowering estate taxes. Spouses can create A-B trust provisions (discussed on page 149), either through a will or a living trust, for estate tax planning. Gifting to family members, charities or others can help reduce tax burdens. Those with large estates should consult an ethical attorney knowledgeable about current tax laws to help save estate taxes.

Surviving spouses can **disclaim** certain amounts of estate assets to reduce the size of their own estates. Some wills contain disclaimer provisions that place the disclaimed assets into a trust. The surviving spouse can use the income and principal of the disclaimer trust, but is not considered the owner of the trust assets by the Internal Revenue Service (IRS). When the surviving spouse dies, the assets in the trust pass to named beneficiaries of the trust. Heirs, other than the surviving spouse, who do not wish to claim an inheritance can also disclaim. In this case, the disclaiming heir would be treated as if he or she died before the decedent. The disclaiming heir's share would pass to the other heirs listed in the will, to the children of the disclaiming heir, depending on what the will said, or through intestate succession (discussed on page 121) if there were no will.

The IRS and New Mexico have created detailed rules for making valid disclaimers, discussed more on page 196. Disclaimers under federal tax law must be **in writing** and made **within nine months** of the death of the decedent. If you have a taxable estate, hiring a tax attorney who has specialized knowledge in estate and tax planning could save your estate thousands of dollars in taxes.

Signing the Will/Two Witnesses Required

You must **sign** and **date** your will in front of **two witnesses**. To be valid, a will **must** be witnessed by two people. Although New Mexico does not require witnesses to wills to be eighteen, using adult witnesses is advisable. New Mexico law allows "interested witnesses" to sign a will. "Interested witnesses" may include heirs, devisees, children, spouses and others who might benefit from a will. **However, using interested witnesses is not recommended**. It is better to use friends, neighbors or staff at an attorney's office as witnesses to avoid any hint that you are being influenced by your beneficiaries in making your will. If only one witness signs, the will is not valid. Furthermore, New Mexico law requires that the witnesses must both be present to see the person sign the will. Then the witnesses must sign the will in the presence of the person making the will and in the presence of each other. You cannot sign your will and then take it around to your neighbors to sign as witnesses.

If you cannot sign your name, **you may not sign an "x" instead of your name.** New Mexico law, however, allows you to direct someone to sign for you. Again, the person signing for you and the witnesses must all be in the same room at the same time and watch each other sign the will.

Notarizing a Will and Other Documents

New Mexico law does not **require** a will to be notarized, but most attorneys who prepare a will for you also notarize it. To make the will harder to challenge and to avoid having to locate witnesses at a later date, many wills are signed in the presence of a notary public. When you and the witnesses sign the will in the presence of a notary public, the will is considered **self-proved** under New Mexico law. New Mexico law requires that certain language be included in a will to make it self-proved.

This book discusses signing documents, such as wills, trusts, deeds and powers of attorney, in the presence of a notary public. New, stricter laws governing notaries took effect on July 1, 2003. A $10,000 surety bond is now required of all notaries for their four-year term.

The most important job of a notary public is to verify that the person signing the document is who they claim to be and personally signed the document in the notary's presence. The person signs the document, the notary signs the notarial certificate, and then the notary either seals an impression on the document or stamps it with a rubber stamp approved by the Secretary of State. From a practical standpoint, an inked rubber stamp photocopies much more easily than a seal impression.

Do not be offended if a notary asks for identification. The notary is doing his or her job correctly. It is also the notary's responsibility to decide whether a person is signing willingly and seems competent to sign.

Notaries should never notarize a document that was not signed in their presence. Under the revised notary law, those who violate this requirement can be convicted and fined up to $1,000, or imprisoned for up to six months, or both.

In New Mexico notaries may perform the following notarial acts:

❑ Acknowledgments;
❑ Oaths and affirmations;
❑ Jurats;
❑ Copy certifications; and,
❑ Other acts allowed by law.

New Mexico notaries may not perform marriages.

Notaries public shall:

❑ Be New Mexico residents;
❑ Be eighteen or older;
❑ Read and write English;
❑ Have no felony convictions; and,
❑ Not have had a notary public commission revoked during the past five years.

The revised law governing notaries contains detailed provisions about their duties and obligations. Although the law does not require it, a notary might want to keep a journal of all notarial acts, along with the date, title of the document and names of the people whose signatures were notarized.

The law also sets fees that notaries can charge As of July 1, 2003, a notary can charge a maximum fee of $5.00 for each acknowledgment, oath, or jurat. If a notary charges more than $5.00 per seal or stamp, ask if the notary is aware of the notary laws that regulate fees. Some notaries charge no fee, especially if they work at businesses that provide free notary services to customers.

The Secretary of State oversees notary appointments, which expire after four years. The application fee increased to $20 on July 1, 2003. Application forms are available on line at **www.sos.state.nm.us/notaryinfo.htm**. For more information or to obtain a pamphlet about notary requirements, call the Secretary of State toll-free at 1-800-477-3632.

New Mexico Statutory Will Act

The 1991 New Mexico legislature passed the Uniform Statutory Will Act. The Uniform Statutory Will is **not** a do-it-yourself document. The Act is ten pages long, quite complex and contains provisions for creating a will and a trust. However, the Act does not conform to long-standing New Mexico law on wills. For example, the Act lists the share of the surviving spouse as the entire statutory will estate *if there are no surviving children*. If there are surviving children, the surviving spouse receives the home and non-investment personal property and "the greater of one hundred fifty thousand dollars ($150,000) or one-half of the balance of the statutory-will estate" and "an interest in the remaining portion of the statutory-will estate, including any property that would pass under . . . this paragraph but disclaimed by the surviving spouse, in a trust upon the terms set forth in [another section] of the Uniform Statutory Will Act."

Identifying who might benefit from this Act is difficult. Certainly the Act is inappropriate for single people and is probably inappropriate for married people with adult children. Perhaps the Act is intended for married people with minor children. The problem with the language is that often spouses intend for the surviving spouse to inherit **all** of the property. Why this Act gives half to the surviving spouse and the other half to a trust for the spouse and children is unclear. **Before you sign a will created under the New Mexico Statutory Will Act, make sure you understand what the will does with your property.** This Act may well create more problems than it solves.

Where to Store Original Will

You should store your will in a safe place that is accessible to your personal representative. Giving the personal representative a copy of the will is also advisable. Many people keep their original wills in a bank safe deposit box. If you fully trust your personal representative, you might consider adding the personal representative's name to your safe deposit box as a tenant so that your personal representative can retrieve legal documents and titles easily upon your death. Adding another person as a joint tenant on a safe deposit box could mean that person owns all of the contents of the box upon your death. If this is not your intention, ask the bank if there is a way to give another person the right to access your box without creating a joint tenancy.

If the safe deposit box has no joint tenant, New Mexico law states that the bank shall permit "the spouse, a parent, an adult descendant or a person named as an executor in a copy of a purported will" of the decedent to open and examine the contents of a safe deposit box leased by the decedent. A very similar law exists for credit unions.

Your personal representative or other person can ask the bank to open the safe deposit box in the presence of an officer of the bank. The personal representative or other person may need the will, a deed to a burial plot or an insurance policy and may remove those items without a court order. The bank should release those items after the person seeking the documents signs a receipt listing the items that are removed.

Testators should store a copy of their will outside of the safe deposit box and tell their personal representative where that copy is. Taking the copy to the bank or credit union should help obtain access to the box.

The bank should not release any other documents until the court appoints a personal representative for the decedent's estate. If the will is in the safe deposit box and the bank refuses to release the will, the personal representative, through an attorney, can apply for a court order authorizing the bank to release the will. The bank shall also permit access to any person named in a court order for the purpose of opening and examining the contents of a safe deposit box.

A court order should be unnecessary if one follows the procedures set out in the law. People might ask their banks or credit unions what the policy is regarding retrieving wills from safe deposit boxes.

New Mexico law also allows you to deposit a will with the clerk of the court for safekeeping during your lifetime. However, problems arise with this method if: (1) you want to remove the will from the court to make changes, (2) you later revoke the will, but fail to remove the old will from the court, or (3) no one knows the will is there.

Some attorneys will keep the original wills of their clients for safekeeping. If a bank is named personal representative, the bank may agree to keep the original. No matter where you store your original will, the important thing is that family members and your personal representative know where the will is. **You do not have to reveal the contents of the will, but you should definitely reveal its location.**

Destroying Old Wills

Most people destroy an old will after they have signed a new will. Destroying old wills prevents problems that would occur if someone found the old will instead of the new will. If you feel your will may be challenged in the future, keeping an old will as evidence of your intent or for historical purposes may be wise. Marking through this old will or writing "revoked on (date) " will ensure that whoever finds it knows it is not your most recent will. A typical will leaves all assets to the spouse, then states that if the spouse does not survive, the children inherit equal shares of the assets. Under these ordinary circumstances, destroying old wills is desirable.

Is a Handwritten Will Valid?

A handwritten will is valid in New Mexico as long as it was properly executed, that is, (1) signed by you or signed by someone you directed who was in your presence, and (2) attested to in your presence by two witnesses who also sign the document. A handwritten will that is signed by you and **only one witness** is **not** valid.

A handwritten will that is signed by you and two witnesses is different from a **holographic** will that is handwritten and signed only by you and **one or no witnesses**. Holographic wills are generally invalid in New Mexico. A holographic will might be valid in New Mexico, however, if before moving to New Mexico you signed the holographic will in a state where holographic wills are valid.

Who Gets My Property if I Have No Will?

Many people believe that dying without a will means the state will take everything. This rarely happens. **Intestate** means dying without a valid will. Sometimes a person has a will that is valid as to some property, but invalid as to other property. Any property not disposed of by a will is called the intestate estate. A person's estate will pass to the state *only if* no takers exist under New Mexico's laws of **intestate succession**.

New Mexico's laws of intestate succession list who inherits the property if no valid will exists. The following charts illustrate New Mexico's laws on intestate succession and show what will happen to your property if you have no valid will.

Chart 1
Surviving Spouse's Share of Decedent's Intestate Estate
(no valid will, surviving spouse)

Type of Property	*Who Receives Property*
Separate Property: property in deceased spouse's name only, such as gifts, inheritances, property acquired before the marriage or property agreed to be separate by both spouses.	If no surviving children, surviving spouse takes all of the deceased spouse's separate property. If there are surviving children, surviving spouse takes ¼ of the deceased spouse's separate property and children take remaining ¾ share in equal shares if all children are alive. If a child has died, the deceased child's children, if any, would split the deceased child's share.
Community Property: property acquired by the spouses during the marriage other than separate property.	Community property belongs ½ to surviving spouse and ½ to deceased spouse; the deceased spouse's ½ share of the community property passes to the surviving spouse.

Chart 2, Intestate Heirs of Single Individual Who Dies
(no valid will, no surviving spouse)

Categories of Surviving Heirs	*Who Inherits the Property*
Spouse alive.	See Chart 1.
No surviving spouse, but surviving children.	Children inherit equal shares of estate. If one child has died, that child's share passes to his or her children.
No surviving spouse or children, but surviving parents of decedent.	Parents inherit equal shares of estate if both survive; or to the surviving parent.
No surviving spouse, children or parents, but surviving brothers and sisters.	Brothers and sisters inherit equal shares of estate. If one sibling has died, that sibling's share passes to his or her children, if any, and, if none, to the other siblings.
No surviving spouse, children, parents, or siblings, but surviving grandparents.	½ to paternal grandparents and ½ to maternal grandparents, but if not alive, to even more distant relatives.
Absolutely no living relatives.	Decedent should have done a will leaving property to friends, charity, etc., but if not, the state gets the property.

Chart 3, Decedent has Valid Will, Spouse or No Spouse	
Title on Property	*Who Receives Property*
Property in decedent's name only.	The will controls to whom the property passes.
Property in decedent's name and anyone else's name.	The surviving named person(s) on the property receives all of the property (this result is discussed in more detail on page 101).

If you do **not** intend for one of your children, a sibling or other relative to inherit, you **must** have a will that clearly states your intentions. If you do not have a valid will, the charts demonstrate how your property will pass. If you did not leave a valid will, the child or relative you wished to disinherit will receive a share of your assets despite your wishes. New Mexico's law on intestate succession only provides for blood relatives, so if you wish to leave a bequest to in-laws or friends, a will is also necessary.

"I've Moved from Another State" or "My Will is Thirty Years Old."

New Mexico law states that a written will executed in another state or country before moving to New Mexico is valid as long as the will was valid in the state or country in which the will was executed. This means that even if your will would not be valid under New Mexico law, if it was valid where you made it, New Mexico's courts will honor it.

Nevertheless, reviewing old wills or wills made in another state is wise. You should consider updating very old wills (over ten or twenty years old) even if the terms remain the same. An updated will shows that you have recently considered your estate plan and chosen a particular way to distribute it. Updating old wills is not required and a will executed many years ago remains valid. Divorce or annulment automatically excludes the ex-spouse from inheriting under the terms of a will, POD, TOD or other beneficiary accounts, or from serving as a personal representative. Legal separation has no effect on a valid will. Updating a will after you divorce or annul a marriage is probably wise, especially if you want to provide for your ex-spouse in the will.

Should I Include Burial Instructions in My Will?

Including burial or cremation instructions in your will may do no good because often no one looks at your will until after the funeral. To ensure that your wishes about burial or cremation are followed, you should write instructions in a separate document. Give copies of the instructions to your children or other responsible parties. You might choose to include burial or cremation instructions in your will **and** create a separate statement summarizing your wishes. You may also consider buying a prepaid funeral insurance plan, but make sure the company with whom you do business is reputable. The longer a company has been in business, the more likely it is that the company is reputable.

Individual May Authorize Own Cremation

Prior to April 1993, if you wanted to be cremated rather than buried, the mortuary required your *next of kin* to sign permission. This requirement angered or distressed many people who believed they should have the right to determine the disposition of their own body. By having the next of kin sign cremation authorization forms, the mortuaries were protecting themselves from possible lawsuits by family members who may not have wanted a cremation.

The 1993 New Mexico legislature passed a law that allows an individual to authorize his or her own cremation in a will or a separate written statement either signed by the individual and notarized **or** signed by the individual and two witnesses. Funeral homes, crematories and others are immune from liability for relying on the statement. If you put your wishes in the proper written form, funeral homes and others can no longer require next of kin to sign permission for your cremation. Discussing your wishes with your immediate family members may still prevent future problems. A sample cremation form is on page 125.

If you do not leave written instructions, but still wish to be cremated, the law allows your next of kin to give permission. If you are married, your spouse is your next of kin. If you have no spouse, a **majority** of your surviving adult children must sign the authorization form. If you have no spouse or children, a **majority** of your surviving siblings must sign. If you have no next of kin, someone close to you who is familiar with your wishes may sign permission for your cremation. The more you talk about your wishes, the more likely it is that your family will follow your wishes.

Changing a Will

Often a person has a valid will and just wants to modify the appointment of a personal representative, change a beneficiary or include a change in marital status. Some people take their original will, cross out the old language and write in the changes. **Don't do this!** These changes would not be valid because they were not signed by you in the presence of witnesses. The beneficiaries of the will would probably face a long and expensive court procedure to straighten things out.

The correct way to change a will is to sign a **codicil** (amendment) to the will. The codicil should: (1) identify the will that is being amended; (2) state your name and the date the will was signed; (3) specify in detail what changes are being made; and (4) state which sections of the will remain in effect.

The codicil must be executed in the same manner as a will. This means that you must sign and date the codicil in the presence of two witnesses who also sign the codicil. New Mexico law does not require the codicil to be notarized, but notarizing the codicil is recommended.

If you have several changes to make, preparing a codicil may take as much time as preparing a new will. If you already have several codicils to your original will, you may prefer to create a new will instead of yet another codicil. New Mexico law does not prohibit a person from adding a codicil to a will that was prepared and executed in another state. However, many attorneys prefer to prepare a new will rather than update a will made in another state.

Revoking a Will

New Mexico law states that you may revoke a will by: (1) creating a subsequent will that revokes the previous will; or (2) performing a revocatory act, such as burning, tearing, canceling, obliterating or otherwise destroying the will with the purpose of revoking the will. You can also direct someone else to burn, tear or otherwise destroy the will in your presence. If a subsequent will does not expressly revoke a previous will, the new will still controls if it disposes of all of the estate. If not, more evidence of your intent is required. New Mexico law does not say that you must be "of sound mind" to revoke a will, but a court would probably rule that you need to understand what you are doing when you revoke a will.

Undue Influence

Unfortunately, sometimes a beneficiary of a will exerts **undue influence** over the person who is making the will. The beneficiary may encourage the person making the will to leave all or the bulk of an estate to him or her. The beneficiary may feel justified in excluding other children or beneficiaries because he or she cared for the person physically or financially. Or the beneficiary may simply be greedy.

Undue influence can also exist between couples. One spouse may wish to leave a certain gift to one beneficiary, while the other spouse may have a different idea. Worse yet, the couple may go to an attorney who prepares wills for both individuals. Then one spouse returns to the attorney behind the other one's back and attempts to change the will. At this point, because the attorney represented both people, the attorney has a **conflict of interest** and should not assist the one spouse to change the will behind the other's back.

Some people are more susceptible to undue influence than others. An older, frail person may become very dependent on someone and allow that person to control his or her life. The best way to avoid having someone make you do something in your will that you do not want is to insist on seeing your attorney alone. If you allow the beneficiary to participate in making your will, you are giving up control over affairs that are rightfully yours. If the beneficiary insists on keeping the will "as a secret just between you and me," things probably are getting out of your control. If a relative, friend or anyone else pressures you to give a large amount of your assets to one person while excluding others, you may be being unduly influenced. If you suspect that a family member, friend or neighbor is being unduly influenced by another, you might consider talking with the person or, in extreme cases, contacting Adult Protective Services (part of the state Human Services Department) in your area.

A will is a very personal document and should reflect your true wishes. If you **intend** to omit certain children or other beneficiaries, discuss this with your attorney. As mentioned previously, you have **no obligation** to leave your assets to your children. But if you mean to omit them from your will, you should be very careful in drafting your will.

New Mexico courts have decided several cases that involve undue influence and wills. Sometimes the court has set aside the will and given the assets to the omitted children or other relatives. In other cases the court has found that the will was valid and was not made under the influence of another person. Each case has different facts and different resolutions. A good attorney can help you set up your will according to your wishes and can also prevent future problems.

Loaning Assets Before Your Death (Advancement)

Sometimes a person will loan or advance money to one child during life. A loan or advance is different from a **gift**. The person making the loan or advance usually wants to offset the loan or advance in the will by reducing the recipient's share of the assets to be received at death. The will (or a separate writing like an IOU) should state clearly that an advance was made to the beneficiary. The donor or the beneficiary can sign the writing. New Mexico law states that the property advanced is valued as of the time the beneficiary received it or as of the time of death, whichever occurs first.

If the donor intended an advancement to the beneficiary, the beneficiary's share of the estate would be offset by the amount of the advancement. If the donor calls the lifetime distribution a **gift** and there is a shortfall of assets in the estate, the recipient may not be obligated to repay the other beneficiaries. If the donor calls the lifetime distribution a **loan** or **advancement**, the beneficiary would probably have to pay the estate back.

Costs of Wills

The costs of wills depend on: (1) the size of the person's estate; (2) whether special circumstances exist, such as second marriages, taxable estates, special needs children, etc.; (3) where you live (in Santa Fe, Albuquerque and Las Cruces, wills probably cost more); and (4) whom you choose to prepare the will, i.e., small firm, large firm, clinic, experienced or new attorney.

The cost of wills is a controversial topic. Some people insist that a will should cost $20 to $50. In smaller communities, some attorneys may provide a will for $100 or $150. Other attorneys may charge $300 to $500 for a simple will and more for a complex will. Many attorneys do not just prepare a will for someone. They examine all of the person's assets; check the titles to all assets; and talk about living wills, powers of attorney and estate planning with the client. This process takes time, for which the attorneys must charge. Other attorneys may not be as thorough. The basic rule that "you get what you pay for" also applies to wills. If you want a more thorough examination of your affairs and wishes, you should be prepared to pay more.

Do I Need an Attorney to Prepare My Will?

People who attempt to write their own wills may create more problems than they solve. Many legal cases exist where a will drafted by the testator fails or is so unclear that his wishes cannot be carried out. As part of the process of drafting a will, you should check all of the titles to your real property (houses, land or ranches), motor vehicles, bank accounts, stocks/bonds, mobile homes and other assets to make sure the property is held the way you want. A good attorney will check all the titles to all of your assets and may notice mistakes in your titles or may ask questions you did not think of when you considered preparing your own will. For example, often you may **intend** to will all of your assets in equal shares to your children. Your attorney may notice that you have put only one child's name as a joint tenant on your bank account, home or motor vehicle. **As mentioned previously, joint tenancy property passes directly and automatically to the surviving joint tenant and is not affected by a will.** This same principle applies to life insurance policies, individual retirement accounts and other documents that name a beneficiary. The named beneficiary will receive the proceeds **even if your will states otherwise.**

Trouble may arise if you try to put conditions on passing property to beneficiaries, but these conditions may not be legal. Or you may leave property to a person who dies before you. Failure to name alternate beneficiaries or to update your will could cause problems. If the court is unable to interpret your instructions, your will may be declared invalid. Worse yet, you may write something you think is clear, but it is interpreted in a way that is contrary to your wishes.

The more assets you own, the more sense it makes to have a professional examine your estate and prepare your will. A properly prepared will is an investment against legal snarls. The purpose of this book is not to teach you how to do your own will, but to give you information about things you may not have thought about. This book may also help you formulate questions to ask a lawyer whom you might hire to prepare your will. Preparing your own will may rank up there with defending yourself in the courtroom. A wise person said long ago that those who defend themselves have fools for clients. People who try to save a little money by preparing their own wills may also have fools for clients, or at least they may create big headaches for surviving spouses or beneficiaries. If an attorney prepares your will, you have someone to blame other than yourself if something goes wrong.

Having a will ensures that your wishes about personal representatives, distribution of assets and other matters are in writing. The process of preparing for a will may cause you to examine and update your financial affairs. Checking title to all assets may prove extremely valuable. While a will does not avoid a probate proceeding, a will does help ensure that the probate will follow your wishes.

5

TRUSTS IN NEW MEXICO

The media have given a lot of publicity to trusts. If one has a will, does one need a trust? Do trusts avoid probate? Are trusts better than wills? Should everyone have a trust? How does one transfer property into a trust? Can trusts help with tax planning?

Trusts[1] are legal documents that set out provisions for the management of property and for the distribution of property upon someone's death. A person (called the **settlor**, **trustor** or **grantor**) creates a trust, transfers assets into the trust and then may choose to manage the trust. The manager of the trust is called the **trustee**. If the settlor serves as the initial trustee and later becomes incapacitated, a **successor trustee** manages the trust. Upon the settlor's death, the assets remaining in the trust pass to **beneficiaries** named in the trust document.

Many types of trusts exist, including trusts for minor children, insurance trusts, supplemental needs trusts for disabled individuals eligible for state or federal benefits, education trusts for grandchildren or others, trusts for the care of an animal, charitable trusts and tax planning trusts. This chapter will discuss testamentary trusts, which are trusts included as part of a will, and simple living trusts

---

[1]New Mexico's law on trusts, the Uniform Trust Code, appears in the New Mexico Statutes Annotated, Sections 46A-1-101 through 46A-11-1104. These statutes are available at the University of New Mexico School of Law Library (Albuquerque), the New Mexico Supreme Court Library (Santa Fe), the New Mexico State University Library located in Branson Hall (Las Cruces) and at various attorneys' offices. You may also purchase copies of these statutes directly from the New Mexico Compilation Commission, PO Box 15549, Santa Fe NM 87506; (505) 827-4821.

(also called revocable trusts or revocable living trusts). A properly drafted revocable living trust can avoid **probate** (court proceeding to pass property to beneficiaries). Other, more complex trusts are outside the scope of this book.

Testamentary Trusts

A testamentary trust can be included as part of your will and takes effect **only upon your death**. Testamentary trusts are used to:

1. Manage and distribute property to children, grandchildren or others who are under a certain age. In this instance the trustee would manage the child's property until the child reached a certain age. Some people select age eighteen (the age of majority in New Mexico), others select age twenty-one or twenty-five, yet others give a portion of the assets to the child at two or three different ages.
2. Manage and distribute property to someone who has a physical or mental handicap.
3. Manage and distribute property for a certain purpose, such as to pay for the education of a child, grandchild or other individual.
4. Provide income and, under certain circumstances, principal, for a surviving spouse with the remainder going to children from another marriage.
5. Reduce estate tax on a surviving spouse's estate.
6. Provide financial management and income to a beneficiary who is incapable of handling financial matters.

Revocable living trusts, discussed below, can also accomplish these goals.

New Mexico law also allows you to make a devise or bequest in your will to a trustee of a trust (this means the trust becomes a beneficiary of your will when you die). The trust must be identified in your will and must exist as a written document. Upon your death, the will distributes your assets, or some part of your assets, into the trust to be held, managed and distributed by the appointed trustee according to your instructions.

Uniform Trust Code

In 2003 the New Mexico legislature passed the Uniform Trust Code (UTC), which governs trust documents in New Mexico. The UTC contains many provisions about creating and managing a trust, as well as provisions regarding trustees' duties and liabilities. The UTC applies to express (written) trusts, charitable or noncharitable trusts, and trusts created pursuant to a law, court judgment or decree. The UTC refers to the person making the trust as the **settlor**.

The UTC states that the mental capacity for creating a trust is the same as that required to make a will. This capacity is discussed on page 92.

New Mexico's UTC recognizes trusts made in other states or countries. If a trust's creation complied with the law of the place where it was made, it should be accepted in New Mexico.

Revocable Living Trusts in New Mexico

A **revocable living trust** (sometimes called an *inter vivos* trust) is created during your lifetime. You transfer assets into the trust during your lifetime by changing the title to the assets.

Estate planning attorneys often use this type of trust for clients who wish to avoid probate. Income and principal can be used for the settlor's[2] benefit during the settlor's lifetime, then pass to designated beneficiaries after the settlor dies. This avoids probating the estate, at least for assets that are part of the trust. Any property that is not included as part of the trust could be passed

---

[2]Often spouses or other couples jointly create a trust in both of their names. The term "settlor" as used throughout this chapter may refer to one or more settlors.

through **probate**, a court proceeding to pass property to beneficiaries.[3]

A typical living trust allows you, as the settlor, to serve as trustee, if you wish. You may also remove and appoint successor trustees, add property to or withdraw property from the trust, or revoke the trust. As mentioned previously, if you are the trustee and become incapacitated, your appointed successor trustee manages the assets in the trust for your benefit. The beneficiaries named in the trust receive the trust assets either immediately upon the settlor's death or at a later time specified in the trust document.

As noted above, a settlor must have **capacity** to create a trust. A settlor must also **intend** to create the trust. If the settlor later becomes incapacitated, the trust may serve as an alternative to a conservatorship (conservatorships are discussed in Chapter One), but the trust document should include detailed provisions about how to determine when a settlor is incapacitated. Usually, certification by two physicians, including the attending physician, that the person is incompetent as defined under New Mexico law is sufficient. Requiring a court to determine incapacity defeats one purpose of the trust, which is to provide for an inexpensive transition for management of an incapacitated client's estate.

Settlors create living trusts for a variety of reasons. To determine whether you are a good candidate to create a living trust, consider the questions on page 161. The most typical reasons are to: (1) avoid probating an estate; (2) establish a way to manage property, especially if someone becomes incapacitated; and (3) keep one's financial affairs private. Living trusts do **not** terminate upon incompetency **or** death.

A durable financial power of attorney, discussed in Chapter One, can also provide for management of incapacitated peoples' assets if businesses will accept it. A durable power of attorney does

---

[3]A probate would not be necessary if the property passed through joint tenancy, payable on death accounts, transfer on death accounts, transfer on death deeds, or a beneficiary designation.

not help a person avoid probate. A durable power of attorney costs a lot less than a living trust, but **all powers of attorney end upon the death of the principal** (the person making the power of attorney). A trust stays in effect even after the settlor dies.

Creating the Trust

The UTC allows certain oral trusts without written documents. The creation of an oral trust and its terms, however, may only be established by clear and convincing evidence. Since oral trusts are difficult to prove and to enforce, this chapter discusses only written trust documents.

The settlor creates a written revocable living trust by signing a trust document (you usually sign once as settlor and once as trustee) **in the presence of a notary public**, who then notarizes the trust document. The settlor or the settlor's attorney must transfer property into the trust to be managed by a trustee (who could be the settlor, a bank, a friend or a relative) for the benefit of a beneficiary or beneficiaries (who could be the settlor during the settlor's lifetime, then the children of the settlor, etc.). The living trust is established and becomes effective during the lifetime of the settlor. Living trusts may be amended at any time and can be terminated at any time by the settlor, as long as the settlor is mentally competent. The power to revoke the trust is essential to avoid liability for gift taxes. Also, property can be transferred in and out of the trust.

Legal title to the assets is held in the name of the trust, so no probate is necessary when the settlor dies. The trust remains in effect when the settlor dies, and the settlor's assets are then distributed according to the terms of the trust. If more than one settlor has created a joint trust, the surviving settlor could change the trust unless the express provisions of the trust state otherwise. After both settlors died, the trust could not be changed unless all beneficiaries consented.

The trustee or successor trustee has the legal authority and power to distribute the assets of the deceased settlor according to the wishes of the settlor expressed by the terms of the trust. The trust should include clear and unambiguous provisions for distributing and managing the estate after the settlor dies, so there will be uninterrupted management according to the settlor's wishes. This might merely involve distributing trust property to beneficiaries and dissolving the trust. Or the trust may provide for long-term management of assets for surviving spouses, minors or beneficiaries with special needs.

Choosing a Trustee

As mentioned above, the **trustee** manages the assets that are transferred into the trust. Often the settlor wants to serve as trustee as long as he or she is able to do so. If the settlor does not wish to manage the assets, the settlor may appoint a bank, trust company, friend or relative to serve as trustee. If the settlor serves as trustee, the settlor will also appoint a successor trustee who will serve if the settlor tires of managing the property, becomes incapacitated or dies. The successor trustee may be a bank, friend or relative.

Choosing a trustee (other than oneself) is a very important decision. Just because someone is related to you does not mean he or she will make a good trustee. Settlors must evaluate the pros and cons of choosing an individual trustee versus a professional corporation. Things to consider before appointing a family member or friend as trustee include:

❑ The age and health of the individual.
❑ The sophistication and knowledge the individual has about taxes, investments and other financial matters.
❑ The general business knowledge of the individual.
❑ The stability and trustworthiness of the individual.
❑ The willingness of the individual to serve.
❑ The location of the individual (out-of-state trustees may find it burdensome to manage a trust).

Things to consider before appointing a professional corporation, such as a bank or trust company, as trustee include:

❑ The size of the corporation.

❏ The experience of the corporation.
❏ The fees involved in managing the trust.
❏ The stability of the corporation.

Sometimes a settlor will decide to appoint a professional corporation and an individual as **co-trustees**. The settlor may also appoint two or more individuals to serve as co-trustees. If the settlor appoints co-trustees, the trust document should clearly define the duties of each trustee. Are both signatures required for all business matters? Can one trustee act without the other? How will disagreements between co-trustees be resolved?

If the trust document does not contain detailed co-trustee provisions, the UTC provides guidance. Under the UTC co-trustees who are unable to reach a unanimous decision may act by majority decision. If one co-trustee is unavailable or incapacitated, the others may continue to act for the estate. The UTC includes "watch dog" provisions for co-trustees. Co-trustees are to exercise reasonable care to "prevent a co-trustee from committing a serious breach of trust" and to "compel a co-trustee to redress a serious breach of trust."

Serving as the trustee of a trust is a big responsibility. Often family members or friends who agree to serve as trustees do not realize what they are agreeing to do. They do not realize they will have to file income taxes, manage investments and prepare accountings. They may not have the bookkeeping or accounting skill necessary to manage the trust properly. They do not realize that they are bound by a **fiduciary duty** to act wisely and prudently. They can be sued if they make bad investments.

Furthermore, beneficiaries may dislike the trustee for making necessary business and financial decisions. After a potential trustee considers all of these factors, he or she may be less willing to serve, especially if he or she is being asked to serve for free.

Banks and trust companies will charge a management fee to serve as trustee, but at least most bank and trust companies are bonded and insured, unlike individuals. On the other hand, banks, trust companies and other corporate fiduciaries are sometimes so large that they cannot give a personal touch to a trust. While their investment and accounting skills may be excellent, those who seek a "family approach" may decide to appoint a family member as trustee.

If the trust document does not specify a trustee's compensation, the UTC entitles a trustee to "compensation that is reasonable under the circumstances." This provision applies to both individual and corporate trustees. If a trust document specifies the compensation, the court can allow more or less if the compensation is unreasonably low or high or if the trustee's duties are substantially different from those originally contemplated. Trustees are also entitled to be reimbursed out of trust property for expenses (with interest as appropriate) incurred in administering the trust.

A settlor must consider many factors before choosing a trustee. Depending on the settlor's goals, the settlor may well decide appointing a professional corporation as trustee is worth the management fee.

Choosing Trust Beneficiaries

Under the UTC most trusts should have a "definite beneficiary." Definite beneficiaries are those who can be ascertained now or in the future. Exceptions to this rule include charitable trusts, trusts for the care of animals, and certain trusts for noncharitable purposes.

Many settlors designate spouses and children as beneficiaries. They may also designate grandchildren, charities, educational institutions, friends and others as beneficiaries. Trust documents designate alternate beneficiaries, in case one or more beneficiaries predecease the settlor. The trust document may also place restrictions on beneficiaries' shares, such as:

- ❑ Receiving trust property or a portion when a beneficiary reaches a certain age;
- ❑ Restrictions on using the trust property, such as for education; or
- ❑ Spendthrift restrictions to protect trust property from a

beneficiary's creditors.

Funding the Trust

After the settlor creates a trust, the settlor must **fund** the trust, which involves transferring assets into the trust. Various companies, such as stock brokerages and banks, have requirements for changing the title. Some will keep a copy of the trust; others will require additional forms. Other documents might include deeds, assignments and transfer statements for corporate stocks and bonds, bills of sale and assignments of life insurance, leases, mortgages, real estate contracts and promissory notes. After the assets are transferred into the trust, the assets should be identified on a **schedule**[4] that is attached to the trust document. The schedule should be updated so that it reflects a current and accurate list of assets that are part of the trust.

Remember that only a funded trust will avoid probate. This means that **only** assets that have been transferred into the trust will pass automatically to the trust beneficiaries when the settlor dies. Unless an exception exists, property not transferred into the trust before the settlor's death will have to pass through a court probate proceeding, which many people wish to avoid. A living trust is especially useful for avoiding a probate of real property, including houses, land and mineral interests, located in another state. Therefore, transferring out-of-state real property into the trust is important.

Titles to Trust Property

For married couples who create a living trust and plan to serve as trustees of the trust, the new title on their accounts will read **"Husband's Name and Wife's Name as Trustees of the Husband's Name and Wife's Name Revocable Trust dated _____."** For single individuals who create a living trust, the

---

[4]Many trust documents call this "Schedule A," and this chapter will do the same.

new title on the accounts will read **"Individual's Name as Trustee of the Individual's Name Revocable Trust dated _____."** This new title would apply to bank accounts, stock accounts, bonds and other assets.

The new title to a **payable on death (POD) bank account** could read **"POD to the trustee of the X Revocable Trust, dated _____."** Not all people wish to put POD bank accounts into a trust. Rather, they prefer to leave POD accounts to certain named beneficiaries. The proceeds in these accounts then pass automatically to the named beneficiaries, as discussed in Chapter Four. Other settlors do not want to put all bank accounts into trust, and may leave their everyday checking account out of the trust. These settlors should make the account POD to the trust or other beneficiary, so that after their deaths, the account would go into the trust without a probate.

Regarding **mobile homes** and other **motor vehicles**, the title must be changed with the Motor Vehicle Division (MVD). You should call the MVD in your area and ask how to proceed. Many people choose **not** to transfer motor vehicles into the trust.

Transferring real estate into the trust requires new deeds to be prepared. **All new deeds must be recorded into the public record in the county where the property is located.** Recording the new deed is important, so that a public record of the transfer of the real estate into the trust exists. New deeds for individuals are drawn up to transfer the property from the individual to **"the Individual's Name as trustee of the Individual's Name Revocable Trust dated _____ and his or her successors in office."** For couples, the new deed will say from Husband and Wife as joint tenants to **"Husband's Name and Wife's Name as Trustees of the Husband's Name and Wife's Name Revocable Trust dated _____ and their successors in office."**

These requirements also apply to **out-of-state real property**. Unless you are very familiar with real estate deeds, seeking the assistance of a title company or attorney in the state where the property is located is advisable to make sure the new deeds comply with state law. Improperly drafted deeds may cloud the title to the real property and require a court procedure to straighten out the title.

Real estate contracts require assignments from the owners to the trustee of the trust. You can ask the escrow company or title company to prepare the appropriate documents for you, but most companies require an attorney to prepare the new assignments.

Some settlors prefer to leave **life insurance policies** out of the trust so that the proceeds will pass directly and immediately to the named beneficiary. This approach might be preferable for those whose estates are nontaxable (below $1,500,000 for single individuals, $3 million for married couples in 2004 and 2005). If you do not wish to take advantage of estate tax planning features of your trust, you may choose not to transfer life insurance into the trust. Be aware, however, that if you die without transferring the life insurance into the trust and the named beneficiary of your policy has also died, a probate will be necessary to pass the proceeds of the life insurance to your estate and into the trust. If you wish to take advantage of tax planning features that may be included in a trust document and want to ensure that no probate is necessary, you would change the beneficiary of the life insurance policy to **"the trustee of the _____ (Name(s)) Revocable Trust dated _____ and their successors in office."**

Other assets that need to be transferred into the trust may include **oil and gas royalty interests**, **limited partnership interests, stocks and bonds**. Transferring household furnishings,[5]

---

[5]Household furnishings can pass to people designated on the tangible list of personal property, discussed on page 119. The list would be prepared in conjunction with the pourover will, discussed on page 155. If a person did not prepare such a list, the heirs would normally divide the furnishings among themselves or hold an estate sale. As long as no one is fighting over the furnishings and the furnishings are not objects of great monetary value, such as antiques, the court (or trustee) does not usually care how the heirs choose to divide them.

homeowner's or automobile liability insurance policies into the trust is not necessary.

A very important point: As soon as you transfer property into the trust, be sure to list the property on the Schedule A attached to your trust document. Schedule A may be the only place that all trust assets are listed, and having Schedule A correct (and updated if you add property later) helps your successor trustee know what property is in the trust. Some people may think that listing the property on Schedule A automatically puts that property into the trust. **This is not true!** You must transfer the property into the trust by changing the title to the property as discussed above. Merely listing the property on Schedule A is not sufficient. **Designate whether each item you list on Schedule A is "community property" or the "separate property of (name)."**

Transferring property into a trust does not happen overnight. Sometimes completing all the transfers takes months. Some people who create trusts want their attorneys to handle all of the transfers. Others may wish to handle the transfers themselves. Most attorneys will insist on at least preparing deeds to real property to make sure the title is changed correctly.

New Mexico law currently allows up to $30,000 of personal property (not real estate) to pass by sworn statements of the successors in interest without a probate proceeding (successors in interest affidavits are discussed in Chapter Six). Therefore, you may not have to transfer absolutely everything into your trust. Just make certain that the value of the personal property left **out** of trust is less than $30,000.

Managing the Trust

After the names on the assets are changed, if the settlor also serves as trustee, the trustee will still sign checks and other documents with his or her own name, but as trustee. At some point, the settlor may no longer wish to manage the trust property. By appointing someone such as a bank as trustee, the settlor would be freed from managing the property. The bank could probably manage the property efficiently and capably, and the bank would handle the tax returns and final accountings when the settlor died. The trust agreement could be set up so that the settlor retained broad powers of control over the property, but allowed the bank discretion in conducting ordinary dealings.

Some settlors prefer to serve as trustee, and then appoint a family member or friend to serve as successor trustee. Others may appoint their accountant. If family members live out of state or are unfamiliar with the duties of serving as trustee, appointing a corporate trustee (bank or trust company) may be wise. A settlor may also wish to appoint a corporate trustee as an objective, neutral party in order to avoid family disputes over management of the trust.

Normally, a trust is not subject to continuing judicial supervision unless ordered by the court.[6] The UTC allows the district court to intervene in the administration of a trust if an interested person so requests.

Responsibilities of Trustees

New Mexico law requires trustees to act honestly, loyally, impartially and prudently. The trustee must follow the terms of the trust and manage the assets properly. If a trustee has special skills or expertise, the trustee should use those special skills or expertise.

A trustee, other than the settlor, may spend trust assets only for the benefit of the settlor(s). Dishonest trustees who spend trust assets on themselves can be sued for improperly converting assets. Risky and speculative investments by the trustee should not occur.[7]

---

[6]Although the UTC does not define "court" as "district court," other provisions of the Uniform Probate Code give the district court exclusive jurisdiction over trust matters.

[7]If you are serving as your own trustee, you are free to invest your money however you wish. If you make a bad investment, you are not likely to sue yourself for mismanagement. But other trustees have certain obligations to follow when managing trust assets.

A court may find that a trustee's bond to secure performance of the trustee's duties is necessary to protect the interests of the beneficiaries or is required by the trust document. The court may modify or terminate a bond at any time.

When a settlor appoints someone other than himself or herself as trustee, the settlor may limit the investments a trustee can make. The trust may state that the trustee may not invest in the stock market. The trust may allow the trustee to invest only in insured certificates of deposit and government obligations. Or the trust may allow the trustee broad discretion in managing the trust assets.

The UTC requires trustees to keep adequate records of the administration of the trust and to keep qualified beneficiaries "reasonably informed about the trust." Most trust documents require the trustee (other than the settlor) to provide an annual (or more frequent) accounting to the settlor and to others the settlor might designate, including beneficiaries. The UTC also requires a trustee to keep trust property separate from the trustee's own property.

Establishing a management committee to advise the trustee can also provide some oversight and accountability. While both the trust document and the law limit the powers of the trustee, as a practical matter, the trustee has enormous power. **Appointing a trustworthy person as trustee is critical.** The legal right to sue the trustee for improper investments, fraud and other reasons, may be worthless if the trustee has spent all of the assets of the trust and has no assets to pay back the trust.

The UTC contains extensive provisions about the office of trustee, the duties and powers of trustees, the liability of trustees and the rights of persons dealing with trustees.[8] Those who agree to serve as trustees should familiarize themselves with the many requirements and duties set out in the law for trustees.

---

[8]These trustee provisions appear in the New Mexico Statutes Annotated, Sections 46A-7-701 through 46A-8-817 and Sections 46A-10-1001 through 46A-10-1012.

Removing a Trustee

The UTC allows a settlor, co-trustee or beneficiary to request the court to remove a trustee. The court, on its own initiative, may remove a trustee if the trustee has:

❑ committed a serious breach of trust;
❑ failed to cooperate with other trustees so as to impair the administration of the trust; or
❑ proved unfit, unwilling or failed to administer the trust properly.

The court may also find a substantial change of circumstances or that removal is requested by all of the qualified beneficiaries. If so, the court can find that removing the trustee best serves the interests of all if a suitable successor trustee is available.

Tax Considerations of Trusts

Transferring property into a living trust does not constitute a completed transfer for gift tax purposes and will not remove the property from the gross estate of the settlor. Living trusts will not relieve the settlor from paying income tax, nor do they reduce the amount of income taxes owed by the settlor. Income tax returns must still be filed.

The Internal Revenue Service (IRS) ignores living trusts for income tax purposes, so the trust does not need a separate tax I.D. number *as long as the settlor is both the settlor and the trustee.* If the settlor is serving as **co-trustee** with another person or entity, the trust would not need a separate tax number. **If the** settlor **and trustee are different people, the trust must obtain a tax I.D. number**[9] **of its own.** Income tax returns generally must be filed by the trustee if the gross trust income for the year exceeds $600.

If the settlor and trustee are one and the same person, the trustee would file a regular IRS Form 1040 income tax return,

---

[9]This number is called an Employer Identification Number (EIN), but is also used for trusts and estates.

using his or her social security number as the identifying number for the trust. If the settlor is a co-trustee with a third party, the trustees would also file the usual Form 1040 and use the settlor's social security number. Special IRS regulations describe the methods of reporting income taxes of the trust. If the trustee is an individual or corporate trustee who is **not** the settlor, the trustee (using the trust I.D. number) would file income tax IRS Form 1041 to report income earned by the trust. If the trustee paid out income to the settlor or other beneficiary, the settlor would also file the usual income tax Form 1040. Although the additional return is required, no additional income tax is due.

When someone dies, one must calculate the fair market value of the decedent's gross estate on the decedent's date of death. This means that the value of the estate includes the value of assets that pass through the probate, as well as the value of joint tenancy property, payable on death accounts, transfer on death deed property, life insurance proceeds, retirement accounts, trust property and all other assets that pass outside of a probate. While these assets do **not** have to be probated, their value is calculated to determine if the estate owes any estate tax. If the total value of the estate is less than $1,500,000, no estate tax should be due. As discussed on page 114, this $1,500,000 figure increases over the next several years.

Depending on the value of a settlor's gross estate, a living trust might include estate tax planning provisions.[10] Federal law authorizes the IRS to collect **estate taxes** on certain estates. Estate tax is different from **income tax**. Estate tax planning is normally necessary when a single person's estate or a married couple's combined estate exceeds $1,500,000 in 2004 and 2005. Usually, a federal or state **estate tax return** would only be required if the total value of the decedent's gross estate exceeded $1,500,000. For an estate exceeding $1,500,000, a U.S. Estate Tax Return, Form 706, must be *filed* even if the estate is worth less than $1,500,000

---

[10]Wills can also include estate tax planning provisions.

after deductions. If the value of the estate, minus deductions and inheritances to spouses and charities (called the **taxable estate**), exceeded $1,500,000 (in 2004 and 2005), estate tax would be due.

As noted in Chapter Four, in 2004 and 2005 estate tax rates start at 45% of the amount over $1,500,000 and rise to a maximum of 48% in 2004 and a maximum of 47% in 2005 for amounts over $2 million. Estate tax is also "tax inclusive," which means that the tax itself is included in the estate tax base, so the estate ends up paying a tax on the tax. Finally, preparing estate tax forms costs money. However, with proper planning, married couples whose estate totals $3 million in 2004 and 2005 ($1,500,000 per spouse) or less can usually avoid paying any estate tax.

The IRS allows certain deductions for funeral expenses, debts and contributions to charity[11] to offset the value of the estate. The IRS also allows **married couples** an **unlimited marital deduction.** The unlimited marital deduction means that a spouse can pass all of the assets to the surviving spouse without paying any estate taxes when the first spouse dies. Deferring the payment of estate tax may sound like a good idea. But if a couple's estate exceeds $1,500,000 in value, giving all the couple's assets outright to the surviving spouse could result in a large estate tax bill when the second spouse dies.

A better idea is to incorporate tax planning techniques into the trust document. With proper drafting, a will or trust can enable a married couple to pass $3 million to beneficiaries without paying any estate tax. Use of the A-B trust is one way to minimize estate tax and gift tax obligations.

A-B Trusts

Married couples with estates over $1,500,000 in value or who are in second marriages may benefit from an A-B Trust. In an A-B

---

[11]Remember that gifts to charity are deducted from the gross estate when calculating estate tax liability. See pages 97 and 108 for more on gifting to charities.

Trust, the couple's assets are in one trust until one spouse dies. At the death of the first spouse, the trustee creates two trust shares, an A Trust and a B Trust. The A Trust is the survivor's trust (one client told me A stands for "above ground"). The B Trust is the decedent's trust (the client said B stands for "below ground"). Part of the couple's assets is in the A trust; the other part of the assets is in the B trust. The B trust becomes **irrevocable.** The surviving spouse **cannot** change the beneficiaries or other aspects of the B Trust. Because the UTC expands the rules about when a trust can be amended or revoked, careful drafting of an A-B trust is crucial to ensure that both settlors' wishes are honored when the first spouse dies.

The A-B trust is useful in protecting a couple's assets over $1,500,000 from estate tax. The beauty of the A-B trust is that the assets in the irrevocable B (decedent's) trust can be *available* to the surviving spouse. The B trust serves as a **credit shelter trust** to protect up to $1,500,000 of assets from being counted for estate tax liability. The credit shelter trust may allow the income generated by the B trust to go to the surviving spouse and the principal of the trust to be tapped for the spouse's health, education, maintenance and support. Typically, when the second spouse dies, the assets in the B trust pass to the children or other named beneficiaries.

If drafted properly, the IRS does not consider the assets in the B trust to be part of the estate of the surviving spouse. These assets are not included in valuing the surviving spouse's estate for determining estate tax liability, yet the surviving spouse may be able to use the assets. This arrangement is the best of both worlds—passing up to $3 million free of estate taxes and having use of all of the money.

An A-B Trust is also useful for couples who wish to leave their own assets to children from another marriage. At the death of the first spouse, the assets would be put into the A trust and B trust. The B trust should become irrevocable and the beneficiaries of the B trust would be the children from the first marriage. The surviving spouse could use the income (and principal if the trust so stated) from the B trust, but upon the surviving spouse's death, the children from the first marriage would receive the proceeds of the B trust.

Some couples may worry that, at their death, the surviving spouse will remarry and the new spouse will get all of the assets. An A-B trust could provide that one-half of the assets pass into the irrevocable B trust (but no more than $1,500,000) and pass to the couple's children. This would protect at least half of the assets if the surviving spouse remarried.

Note: Remember that federal tax law increases the $1,500,000 figure over a period of years and that Congress could change estate taxes rates again in the future. See the chart on page 114 for more information.

Amending/Revoking a Trust

A typical living trust can be amended or revoked at any time. Many trust documents require written amendments and revocations signed by the settlor(s). The UTC also allows a settlor to amend or revoke a trust by a later will or codicil that expressly refers to the trust or by "any other method manifesting clear and convincing evidence of the settlor's intent."

If the trust document has (for some odd reason) been recorded in the office of the county clerk, the amendment or revocation should also be recorded. **The settlor(s) and trustee(s) must sign the original trust document, amendments and/or revocation in the presence of a notary public.**

The UTC states that trusts are presumed to be revocable unless the terms of the trust specifically say that the trust is irrevocable. This is a major change from prior trust law.[12] Therefore, this particular provision regarding presumed revocability does not apply to trusts created before July 1, 2003, the effective date of the UTC.

---

[12]Prior trust law stated that if the terms of a trust were silent about revocation, the trust was deemed irrevocable.

The UTC allows a settlor to revoke or amend a trust that is not irrevocable. If a trustee does not have knowledge of the revocation, however, the trustee is immune from liability for actions taken after the trust was revoked.

If a settlor becomes incapacitated after creating the trust, a guardian, conservator or agent under a durable power of attorney may be able to exercise the power to revoke or amend a trust on the settlor's behalf. Guardians and conservators must first obtain permission from a district court. The power of attorney or trust document must include the specific power for an agent to amend or revoke the settlor's trust.

Under former law an irrevocable trust could not be amended or revoked. One notable provision of the UTC allows a noncharitable **irrevocable** trust to be modified or terminated upon consent of the settlor and all beneficiaries. So irrevocable trusts are no longer truly irrevocable if unanimous consents are obtained to change or end them. Irrevocable trusts are sometimes used in estate planning for people who have taxable estates.

The trustee may conclude that the value of the trust property is insufficient to justify the cost of administering the trust. The UTC allows the trustee of a trust, after notice to qualified beneficiaries, to terminate a trust containing trust property with a total value less than $50,000.

Finally, the UTC allows a district court to modify the terms of a trust to achieve a settlor's tax objectives. The court must act in a way that is "not contrary to the settlor's probable intentions." These changes may have retroactive effect, if the court so orders.

Costs Relating to Trusts

Hiring an attorney to draft a living trust will cost money. If someone other than the settlor (such as a bank) manages the trust, there will be trust management fees. Transferring titles to all property into the trust may cost money. If someone other than the settlor manages the trust, the trustee must give an annual accounting to the settlor and the beneficiaries; this will probably also cost money. There will be fees for filing tax returns while the settlor is alive and after death there will be final accounting costs. These fees together may or may not offset any fees saved by avoiding probate.

A simple living trust for a nontaxable (less than $1,500,000 in 2004 and 2005) estate with no special provisions for handicapped or special needs beneficiaries should take an attorney about ten to fifteen hours to complete. This time estimate may vary, depending on whether the settlor, rather than the attorney, assumes responsibility for transferring assets into the trust. The attorney would also prepare the pourover wills, discussed below. To be thorough, the client should also sign a health care power of attorney, a financial power of attorney and an end-of-life directive. The ten to fifteen hour estimate would normally include these documents. Some attorneys charge a **flat fee** for living trusts and other documents, regardless of how many hours they spend creating the documents.

Legal fees vary greatly, from $500 in rural areas to $1,000 in Albuquerque to up to $2,500 in Santa Fe for a non-taxable trust. Many Albuquerque attorneys will prepare a simple living trust and related documents for between $1,000 and $1,500. A trust for a taxable estate (generally $1,500,000 for single individuals, $3 million for married couples) may cost from $1,200 to $3,000 (up to $3,500 or more in Santa Fe). For people who have very large estates, including out-of-state property, businesses, ranches and other assets, extensive tax planning will be necessary. Preparing a trust for these people could cost thousands of dollars. But hiring an attorney with advanced knowledge in tax matters could save much, much more in taxes.

You are not just paying for the actual legal documents. The attorney will also examine all assets, make recommendations regarding tax planning and tailor the legal documents to your particular needs. The attorney may suggest methods to avoid family conflict and ways to provide for the various needs of beneficiaries. The attorney will meet with you, draft the document, discuss the document with you and revise the document. All of these tasks take time, for which the attorney must charge.

The more organized you are, the less hours the attorney will spend on your case. Have a list of questions to ask the attorney. Write out your goals and wishes regarding the distribution of assets. Organize all of your assets and bring deeds, account statements, lists of investments, broker and accountant's names, etc. to the attorney. Provide the names and addresses of trustees and beneficiaries. If you, rather than your attorney, handle the transfer of most of the assets into the trust, this will also save fees. To make sure that the title is changed correctly, the attorney will probably insist on at least preparing new deeds to transfer real property into the trust.

Advantages of a Living Trust

❑ Does not require the same formalities as executing a will; therefore, easy to change because it does not need witnesses.

❑ Provides privacy, because trusts are not part of the public record; a will becomes part of a probate proceeding and the court file can be reviewed by anyone.

❑ Avoids probate, which will save time, and possibly money; probate costs vary, but anyone who is considering setting up a living trust to avoid probate should ask their attorney to provide a cost comparison between setting up a living trust and probating an estate.

❑ Can be drafted to reduce or eliminate estate tax (a will can also include tax planning provisions).

❑ Provides a good way for a spouse with separate property to pass the property to children from a prior marriage; the trust can provide that upon the death of that spouse, the trustee will continue to hold and manage the deceased spouse's separate property for the benefit of the surviving spouse and upon the death of the surviving spouse, the separate property can then be distributed to the children by the prior marriage.

❑ Offers management protections to a surviving spouse, who can retain control over the trust as long as the surviving spouse is able to do so; if the surviving spouse becomes incapacitated, the trustee can manage the trust funds for the benefit of the surviving spouse.

Disadvantages of a Living Trust

❑ Two title changes for all property; one title change to transfer assets into the trust and another title change at death to transfer property to the beneficiaries.

❑ Trust management fees may equal costs of probate.

❑ Administering the trust may be as complicated as probate.

Pourover Wills

A settlor sometimes fails to transfer all assets into the trust. The settlor may also acquire assets through inheritance, gift, lottery winnings or other means that are not put into the trust. To make sure that these assets are transferred into the trust when the settlor dies, the settlor also signs a "**pourover will**" simultaneously with the trust document. The pourover will provides that any assets remaining outside the trust at the time of the settlor's death "pour over" from the decedent's estate to the trust. This means assets that have not been transferred into the trust prior to the settlor's death will have to be transferred to the trust through a court probate proceeding. Probating assets left out of the trust defeats one of the purposes of the trust, which is to avoid probate. If all of the settlor's property has been transferred into the trust before the settlor dies, the pourover will does not need to be probated, but may be used to distribute personal effects.

Note: One bank trust officer has reported that he has seen some old trusts (around twenty years old) that pour all trust assets back into the estate when the settlor dies. This would mean a probate is necessary to distribute the assets to the beneficiaries. If you have a very old trust, check to make sure this provision is not a part of your trust. If your trust includes this provision, amend your trust to avoid a probate.

Powers of Attorney Recommended, Even If You Have a Trust

Most attorneys who prepare trusts will also have you sign durable financial and health care powers of attorney. A living trust does not cover health care and other personal decisions, but only covers financial matters of the settlor. A bank or trust company that serves as trustee will not be able to make treatment and care decisions for you, but will only be able to pay the bills and expenses of your care. The trustee you name in your trust may not be the same person you would like to make health care decisions, so you should be sure to sign a separate health care power of attorney.

You should also sign a financial or general power of attorney in case the trust document does not cover all financial powers. For instance, a trustee may not have the authority to file health care insurance claims for you; an agent named in a separate financial power of attorney would be able to do so. A financial power of attorney should also authorize your agent to complete the transfer of assets into the trust if you become incapacitated and have not finished the transfer of assets.

As discussed above, an agent appointed by a power of attorney can amend or revoke a settlor's trust, if the power of attorney or trust document specifically grants this power to the agent. If you do not want your agent to have this power, do not include it in your power of attorney or trust document.

Annual Gift Tax Exclusion

One simple tax planning technique is the annual gift tax exclusion. This tax provision allows a donor to make gifts of up to $11,000 per person per year without paying gift taxes or other taxes. A donor may give **more** than $11,000 to anyone in a year, but must file a U.S. Gift Tax Return, Form 709. Recipients of gifts can be children, friends, neighbors, other relatives or anyone else. The IRS does not consider these gifts to be income, and the recipients do not have to declare the gifts on their income tax return.

The donor can give up to $11,000 per person per year to as many people as the donor wishes. Gifts of more than $11,000 per person per year can be made without tax consequences if paid **directly** to persons who provide medical care or for tuition to certain educational institutions.

You cannot retain any control over or place any conditions on gifts you make. Also, **make sure the gift is paid by December 31 in the year the gift is made.** This means checks must be paid by the bank (make allowances for holidays, postal and other delays) before the last day of the year in order to count as a gift in that year. If you write a check that does not clear the bank by the last day of the year, the gift will count for the following year. To be safe, consider giving cashier's checks instead of personal checks toward the end of the year.

The donor **cannot** take an income tax deduction for the gift, unless it is to a qualified charity. Some kinds of property are not subject to the gift tax exclusion, such as certain kinds of life insurance. Transferring property valued at over $11,000 to a living trust does **not** incur gift taxes and does not require Form 709 to be filed. Contributions to qualified charities do **not** incur a gift tax, even if the contribution exceeds $11,000.

The annual gift tax exclusion is a good way to spend down assets, particularly if an estate is worth close to or more than $1,500,000. Keeping an estate below $1,500,000 (in 2004 and 2005) should avoid liability for estate or gift taxes.

The annual gift tax exclusion of $11,000 increases by an amount equal to the cost-of-living adjustment. Increases do not occur every year.

Basis of Property

One thing to consider when giving away assets is the **basis** of the property. The basis of property is its original value at the time of acquisition. At death, the basis of an asset becomes the fair market value at the date of death. This increase in value at death is called the "stepped-up basis". Thus, old stock would acquire a new basis and result in significantly less capital gain (assuming the stock has increased in value since purchase) for the recipient if it were passed on through a will or a trust as a result of a death. When property is passed on as a gift **during someone's life**, rather than at his or her death, the recipient takes the basis of the donor. The following examples illustrate this point:

Example 1: B buys stock for $10 a share. The stock appreciates to $50 a share. B gives the stock to friend C. If C sells the stock, the basis of the stock is $10 a share. C must pay a capital gains tax on the $40 a share profit. B's original basis **carries over** to C.

Example 2: B buys stock for $10 a share. The stock appreciates to $50 a share. B **wills** the stock to C. B dies. B's assets are valued at the fair market value at the date of B's death. When C receives the stock as an inheritance, C's basis is $50 a share, the value on B's date of death. If C sells the stock for $50 a share, C pays no capital gains tax on the sale of the stock. The basis of B's assets is stepped up at B's death.

Some people think that transferring property into a trust will "step up" its basis. **This is not the case**. The IRS only allows the basis of property to be stepped up at death.

In New Mexico, between spouses, if property is held in joint tenancy or as community property, the **entire** basis of the property is stepped up at death.[13] If the surviving spouse sold the home

---

[13]In many non-community property states, only half of the value of joint tenancy property is stepped up at the death of the first spouse. In New Mexico, for joint tenants other than spouses, only half of the value of the property is stepped up at the death of the first joint tenant, assuming each joint tenant paid an equal share of the property.

shortly after the death of the first spouse, the surviving spouse would pay no capital gains tax, even if the home was bought for $10,000 and sold for $200,000.[14] However, one-half of the current value of the joint tenancy asset is included in the decedent's taxable estate at death for purposes of determining if any estate tax is owed. If the property were held in the surviving spouse's sole name, the value of the entire asset would be stepped up again when that spouse died.

Some settlors may move out of state, but may wish to preserve the entire step up in basis awarded to New Mexico spouses. Holding the property in a revocable living trust should ensure that the couple continues to benefit from the New Mexico rules. This is because New Mexico would be the "situs" (legal location) of the trust, and New Mexico's community property and tax rules would apply.

An important exception to the stepped-up basis rule relates to assets that are tax-deferred or have not yet been taxed, such as U.S. savings bonds, certain pensions, IRA's and annuities. These assets are considered **income in respect of the decedent**, discussed on page 109, and are not stepped up at the death of the owner. Since taxes were not paid on these assets, the assets become subject to **income** tax, which must either be paid by the estate or those who receive the property. Consult a knowledgeable tax attorney about these complex rules.

---

[14]A taxpayer may exclude from gross income up to $250,000 of gain from the sale or exchange of the taxpayer's principle residence, during the taxpayer's lifetime. Married couples filing jointly for the year of the sale can exclude up to $500,000 of home-sale gain if certain conditions are met. In the case of unmarried joint owners, according to recent IRS tax regulations, each taxpayer may be allowed to exclude up to $250,000 of gain. With limited exceptions, the homeowner must own and use the home for at least two of the five years before the sale. A vacant parcel of land next to the principal residence may qualify for the exclusion if the land is used as part of the residence and is sold within two years before or after the sale of the principal residence.

Misinformation Provided by Companies that Sell Trusts

In New Mexico several companies, attorneys and others give seminars to various audiences about the advantages of living trusts. Some presenters give very accurate and even-handed information. But some presenters state "facts," such as probating an estate worth $300,000 will cost 10% or $30,000 or property will be tied up in probate for many years. These "facts" should not be true in a routine, uncontested probate.

With a good attorney, probate in New Mexico can be a simple and inexpensive procedure. For estates valued at less than $1,500,000, where no one is fighting over the will, an informal probate may be adequate. For an estate that consists of a house worth $100,000 and $200,000 of stocks and bank accounts, the fees to probate this estate should not be anywhere near $30,000. Assuming no problems arise, probating a simple, nontaxable estate with only a few assets should cost $500 to $2,000, depending on the hourly fee charged by the attorney, guidance needed by the personal representative and other factors.

If you have been charged 10% or $30,000 for probating a simple estate such as this, you should consider filing a complaint with the Disciplinary Board of the Supreme Court, 400 Gold SW, Suite 800, Albuquerque, NM 87102. This board regulates the conduct of attorneys in the state.

Can I Prepare My Own Living Trust?

Some companies provide do-it-yourself trust kits that cost $29.95 or more. Other companies will sell you a simple living trust form for $1,500 (more than many attorneys in New Mexico charge). I do not recommend that anyone prepare his or her own living trust. Understanding the concepts of community property, title to property, tax planning and other aspects is essential to creating a trust document tailored to your specific needs. Filling out forms may seem easy, but understanding the true effect of the words is not so easy. A person should certainly think long and hard before buying a trust prepared out of state that costs more than a trust prepared in state. Having a local attorney to call and ask questions is very valuable.

The larger your estate, the more foolhardy it is to prepare your own trust. The more complex and diverse your assets, the more sense it makes to hire a competent attorney. You should consult the attorney of your choice if you would like to set up a living trust to ensure that the paperwork and transfer of assets to the trust are done properly.

I Did My Own Trust—Now I Want an Attorney to Check It

Sometimes people prepare their own trusts and then worry that everything is not right. They will call an attorney and ask the attorney to review their trust. Most attorneys are reluctant to do so. Attorneys are responsible for the legal work they do. They can be sued for malpractice if they make a big mistake. To ask an attorney to extend their malpractice coverage to a document they did not create is unfair. Do not be surprised if an attorney declines to review your trust.

Other attorneys may agree to review the trust. For this service they will charge by the hour. The attorney may make an alarming number of suggestions to improve the trust. If you pay the attorney to incorporate the changes, you may just as well have paid for a trust created from scratch.

Questions to Ask Before Creating a Trust

1. Have I carefully considered several estate planning options, including wills, how I've titled my property, and trusts?
2. Are my assets titled solely in my name without any beneficiary designations?
3. Does my estate consist of more than a house and bank accounts?

4. Do I want to provide for children from a first marriage?
5. Am I worried about my spouse remarrying and giving my assets to the new spouse?
6. Can I use a trust for tax planning, i.e., is the estate over $1,500,000 (in the year 2004 and 2005)?
7. Do I own real property out of state or in several counties?
8. Do I have minor, dependent or special needs children whose property should be held in trust?
9. Do I wish to use a trust to avoid Medicaid estate recovery liens against my property (relating to nursing home benefits, *see* page 87) or to avoid a court-appointed conservatorship?
10. Am I concerned about Alzheimer's disease or other conditions that may render me incapacitated in the future?
11. Do I want to retain privacy for my financial matters?
12. Do I want to avoid a court probate proceeding?
13. Do I want someone else to manage my assets, if not now, in the future?

If the answer to several of these questions is *yes*, you may be a good candidate to create a living trust. If the answer to most of the questions is *no*, creating a trust may be unnecessary.

Although some attorneys will be happy to sell a living trust to anyone, regardless of the size or complexity of the estate, **a living trust is not appropriate for everyone.** When individuals with simple estates have used payable on death accounts or joint tenancy to avoid probate and have signed powers of attorney to provide for management of their affairs, a living trust is not always necessary.

Trusts for Medicaid Planning

As discussed in Chapter Three, trusts can be used to help with Medicaid planning and/or paying certain health care and nursing home expenses. Please refer to Chapter Three for more details about Medicaid Trusts.

Whether or not to set up a trust depends on how much property you own that requires extensive management. Alternatives are certainly available to make life easier and to avoid trips to the bank to deposit checks. One quite useful and simple alternative would be to arrange for direct deposit to the bank of dividend, interest or social security checks.

Other people prefer to establish a trust tailored to their specific needs. After all assets are transferred into the trust, management is simple. If you become incapacitated, you are assured that the successor trustee will manage your financial affairs in the manner set out in the trust document. If you die, your assets pass fairly quickly to your beneficiaries without a probate. Although trusts are not appropriate for everyone, trusts do provide useful planning and management aspects

6

PROBATING AN ESTATE IN NEW MEXICO

Probate[1] is a court proceeding to distribute a deceased person's property (also called **assets** or **estate**). Not all of a person's property must be probated. As mentioned in Chapters Four and Five, assets held in **joint tenancy, payment on death (POD) accounts, transfer on death (TOD) accounts, transfer on death deeds (TODD), life insurance and other assets with named beneficiaries, and trust property** pass automatically to the named survivor or beneficiary and do **not** pass through a probate proceeding. If **all** of a person's property were held this way, a probate would not be necessary. Individual bank accounts, real property held separately or as tenants in common and certain personal property usually need to be probated in order to pass clear title to the person who will receive the property.

This chapter on probate provides a summary of the probate process. Do-it-yourself probate forms, discussed on page 174, have been approved by the New Mexico Supreme Court. After an individual files a probate, with or without an attorney's help, the court appoints a personal representative[2] to oversee the legal affairs of the decedent.

---

[1]New Mexico's law on probate appears in the New Mexico Statutes Annotated, Sections 45-1-201 through 45-1-404 and Sections 45-3-101 through 45-3-1302. These statutes are available at the University of New Mexico School of Law Library (Albuquerque), the New Mexico Supreme Court Library (Santa Fe), the New Mexico State University Library located in Branson Hall (Las Cruces) and at various attorneys' offices. You may also purchase copies of these statutes directly from the New Mexico Compilation Commission, PO Box 15549, Santa Fe NM 87506; (505) 827-4821.

[2]As defined on page 94, the personal representative is the same as an

Introduction to Probate Terms

A **decedent** (deceased person) may own **real property** (houses, land, ranches, timber and mineral interests still attached to the ground, etc.) or personal property. **Personal property** includes items like bank accounts, stock accounts, retirement accounts, insurance policies, annuities and royalties. These are items of **intangible personal property**. Furniture, guns, jewelry, artwork, vehicles and other household items are **tangible personal property**.

Both real property and personal property may be probated in probate court or district court.

Intestate means dying without a valid will. **Testate** means dying with a valid will. Both intestate and testate estates may be probated in probate court or district court.

As mentioned in Chapter Four, **heirs** are the people who would inherit an intestate estate if there were no valid will. **Devisees** are the people named in a decedent's will to inherit an estate. A person can be both an heir and a devisee.

Probate Estate and Gross Estate

The decedent's **probate estate** is the part of a deceased person's estate that is governed by the provisions of the Uniform Probate Code. The probate estate requires a court probate proceeding to pass that part of the estate to the decedent's heirs or devisees.

The probate estate includes decedent's property, both real and personal, that is titled in decedent's **sole name** or as **tenants in**

---

executor or administrator of your will. The personal representative is responsible for carrying out the terms of your will. If you have no will, the personal representative must distribute your property to your heirs according to New Mexico's intestate laws.

common, discussed in Chapter Four. The probate estate does **not** include property that is held in joint tenancy, trusts, life estates and those assets with beneficiary designations unless the estate, rather than an individual, is named as a beneficiary.

The decedent's **gross estate** includes all property owned by the decedent at the time of death, no matter how titled, including assets that are not subject to probate. The fair market value of the gross estate is used to calculate a decedent's estate tax liability, if any.

To determine the value of the decedent's gross estate, the personal representative should list **all** of the decedent's property, including probate estate assets, joint tenancy property, payable on death accounts, transfer on death accounts, transfer on death deeds, accounts with named beneficiaries and trust property to decide whether the fair market value of the estate exceeds $1,500,000. The first $1,500,000 of a decedent's estate is exempt from estate tax in 2004 and 2005. If the value of the estate exceeds $1,500,000, estate tax may be due to the IRS (*see* page 194).

Probate Procedure in Court

Many people hear the word "probate" and think "takes many years," "costs lots of money," "is very complicated," "must be avoided at all costs." These impressions, while sometimes true, do not apply to many probates. With efficient planning, a routine uncontested probate can be opened and closed in six to twelve months. To open a probate, a lawyer or *pro se* applicant (someone who acts without an attorney's help) files an application with the court, asking the court to appoint a **personal representative** to handle the probate. The application includes a will (if any), a list of the heirs or devisees and information about the person who has died. If the person who died has a valid will, the will probably states who should serve as personal representative. If no one is available to serve, the judge will appoint someone.[3]

---

[3]Most wills state that a personal representative can serve without posting a bond. A bond would provide some monetary protection if a personal

If the probate is opened **informally**, the judge will not hold a hearing but will sign an order appointing the personal representative. If the probate is opened **formally**, **notice** will be given to heirs, devisees and other interested people, and the judge will hold a **hearing** before issuing an order. The court will then issue **Letters of Administration** (if there is no will) or **Letters Testamentary** (if there is a will) to the personal representative. These Letters allow the personal representative to conduct business on behalf of the estate. If bank or stock accounts are involved, the personal representative usually obtains a tax I.D. number from the Internal Revenue Service (IRS). This tax number allows interest earned to be reported to the decedent's estate rather than to the social security number of the decedent or personal representative.

Within ten days of appointment, the personal representative must give Notice to Heirs and Devisees of the Estate (and to anyone who has demanded notice. This is notice that the probate has been filed and a personal representative appointed. In addition to this notice, the personal representative may choose to send a copy of the will and initial probate application to each person entitled to notice. The heirs and/or devisees can opt to receive no further notice of the proceedings by signing a **Waiver of Notice,** which is filed with the court.

A personal representative must give written notice by mail or other delivery to any known creditor and to reasonably ascertainable creditors **within three months** after the personal representative's appointment. A Notice to Creditors may also be published once a week for two consecutive weeks. The Personal Representative may want to publish this Notice to Creditors in order to limit the time an unknown creditor has to file a claim against the estate. Albuquerque has a special legal newspaper for publishing these notices, or they can be published in a regular newspaper.

---

representative did something wrong. Bonds are discussed on page 181.

Creditors whose claims arose before the decedent's death must present claims within two months after the notice was mailed or published, whichever is later, or be forever barred from receiving payment. The creditor presents a claim either to the personal representative or to the court.

Creditors must present claims no later than one year after the decedent's death.[4] Creditors whose claims arose **at or after** the decedent's death generally have four months from the time the claim arises or was performed to present the claim. The personal representative has **sixty days** after the time for original presentation of the claim has expired to allow or disallow the claim. Silence equals allowance of the claim, so personal representatives should be diligent in acting on claims.

The personal representative must pay claims in a certain order. See page 191 for more details.

Certain assets of decedent are exempt from creditors' claims. For example, New Mexico law exempts most life insurance proceeds from creditors' claims.[5]

An **Inventory and Appraisal** of the decedent's property must be prepared **within three months** after the personal representative is appointed. The personal representative must send a copy of the inventory to interested persons who request it and *may* (not required) file it with the court.

Hiring an appraiser to value the decedent's property is not always necessary, but the personal representative should calculate an estimated valuation during the probate proceeding. The personal representative should value the property as accurately as possible because the IRS can penalize those who overvalue assets in an attempt to reduce taxable gains to the beneficiaries. This information will be useful when the property is later sold or passed to beneficiaries.

---

[4]If a personal representative waited one year before starting a probate and a creditor did not start the probate himself/herself within the year, the creditor would probably be unable to collect payment from the estate.

[5]See New Mexico Statutes Annotated, Section 42-10-5 and page 192.

Generally, personal representatives do not need court approval to act on behalf of an estate. An interested person (heir, devisee, creditor, etc.) can, at any time, file a petition with the court asking for a **supervised administration** of the estate. The court may order a supervised administration if it is necessary to protect persons interested in the estate. If this happens, a personal representative would require court approval before acting. Supervised administrations will add to the cost of probate.

Two Kinds of Court and Proceedings

In New Mexico a probate proceeding can be opened in either **probate court** or **district court.** Each of New Mexico's 33 counties has a probate court. There are 13 judicial districts in New Mexico. Each judicial district has a district court, which handles cases for one or more counties within its district.

As mentioned above, a probate may be opened formally or informally. Informal proceedings are filed by an "Application" without prior notice and hearing to interested persons. The judge appoints a personal representative, based on paperwork alone. Formal proceedings are filed by a "Petition" and require notice to all interested persons prior to a hearing to appoint a personal representative.

Probate courts can only accept informal, uncontested probates; the probate court filing fee is $30. Informal probates can be filed in probate court or district court, but formal probates must be filed in district court.

Some people wish to open a probate informally, but close it formally with notice and a hearing to interested persons before closing. This combination would have to be filed in district court. In some New Mexico counties, almost all probates are filed in the district court. No matter which court you use, actual notice must still be given to known or reasonably ascertainable creditors, who have a **two-month** period to file a claim.

Although not required by law, if real property (houses, ranches, land, mineral rights) is involved, some attorneys prefer to file the probate in district court. Also, if a probate is a formal proceeding, is contested, or involves trusts, missing heirs or guardianships, the probate must be filed in district court. The district court's filing fee varies in each district, ranging from $107 to $122.

Jurisdiction: Which Court to File in?

Jurisdiction is the authority for a court to act on a certain matter. Probate courts are courts of "limited jurisdiction," and only have the authority to act over informal probate or appointment proceedings. The probate court may accept informal probate cases and admit wills to informal probate. Probate courts may also informally appoint a personal representative, appoint a special administrator in an informal proceeding, and appoint a successor personal representative, when the original personal representative dies or resigns.

The district court may also do the above things. The probate court has what is known as **concurrent jurisdiction** with the district court to preside over informal probate matters. This means that a person can file an informal probate in either probate court or district court.

Only the district court has jurisdiction over:
❑ formal probate proceedings, including formal closings;
❑ supervised administrations;
❑ estates of missing and protected persons;
❑ protection of incapacitated persons and minors (including guardianships and conservatorships); and,
❑ trusts.

Only the district court can:
❑ approve the sale or encumbrance of property to the personal representative, his spouse, agent or attorney;
❑ appoint someone without the highest priority to serve as personal representative;
❑ make a formal determination as to the validity of a will;
❑ consider admitting a **copy** of a will, rather than an original;

- ❑ preside over a trial in a contested probate matter;
- ❑ hear a "petition for allowance" of a disputed creditor's claim;
- ❑ remove a personal representative for cause;
- ❑ open a probate case more than three years after death when a will exists; or,
- ❑ enter an order restraining a personal representative from acting.

Domicile and Venue

Domicile is a person's usual and permanent place of residence. A person's domicile is important in determining venue, i.e., how to choose the correct court in which to file the probate case. Questions that help determine a person's domicile include:

- ❑ Where is the person registered to vote?
- ❑ Is this their permanent address?
- ❑ Where is their vehicle registered?
- ❑ From what state is their driver's license issued?
- ❑ Is this the place they intend to return to, even if they currently reside elsewhere?
- ❑ From which state do they file their income taxes?
- ❑ Where does the person consider his or her permanent place of residence?

A decedent's will may provide evidence of a decedent's domicile, although it may not if the will was written long ago or when the testator lived in another state. The death certificate states the decedent's domicile. A probate case is usually filed in the court in the county or judicial district where the decedent was domiciled.

Venue means the place where the case should be filed. Which county's probate court or which district court does one use when someone dies? Venue for the first informal testacy or appointment proceedings after a decedent's death is:

(1) in the county where the decedent had his domicile at the time of his death; or

(2) if the decedent was not domiciled in New Mexico, in any

county where property of the decedent was located at the time of his death. ("Property" can mean real or personal property.)

Example 1: Meg dies domiciled in Bernalillo County. All of Meg's property is located in Bernalillo County. Where do you file the Application for Appointment of Personal Representative? The personal representative or his/her attorney must open the case in Bernalillo County Probate Court or Second Judicial District Court.

Example 2: Armando dies domiciled in Bernalillo County. He owns real property in Taos County. No other property requires a probate. Where do you file the Application for Appointment of Personal Representative? The personal representative must open the case in Bernalillo County Probate Court or Second Judicial District Court, and then file a Notice of Administration, discussed on page 188, in Taos County. Some people believe that the personal representative can open the case directly in Taos County, but the laws on venue do not support this.

Example 3: Bertha dies domiciled in Durango, Colorado. All of Bertha's property passes outside of probate, except for property she owns in Socorro County. Where do you file the Application for Appointment of Personal Representative? The personal representative opens the case in the county where the property is located. Therefore, the case may be opened in the Socorro County Probate Court or the Seventh Judicial District Court.

Example 4: Arnold, who is domiciled in California, dies without a will. Arnold's estate requires a California probate, which has already been opened there. But Arnold also owns a piece of real property in Albuquerque, New Mexico. What must the personal representative do? Arnold's Californian personal representative has three options. First, the personal representative could file a "Proof of Authority" in Bernalillo County's Probate Court or Second Judicial District Court, including 1) **authenticated**[6] copies of the California appointment, 2) any

---

[6]Authenticated copies are different from certified copies. To be certified, a

official bond that has been given; and 3) a statement of the domiciliary foreign personal representative's address.[7] Second, Arnold's personal representative could open an informal probate, but would need to modify the language in the do-it-yourself form to indicate that another probate had already been opened. Third, the personal representative could initiate a formal ancillary proceeding in the district court.

Do-it-Yourself Probate Forms

The New Mexico Supreme Court approved do-it-yourself probate court forms for use by the public without the assistance of an attorney. Those who act without an attorney's help are called *pro se* applicants. Some attorneys have started to submit these forms as well.

Copies of the do-it-yourself forms can be obtained:

❑ As packets, sold by the probate courts for $5 per packet;

❑ From the internet, **www.nmcourts.com** (or try **http://www.supremecourt.nm.org/cgi-bin/download.cgi/supctforms/probate** first),[8]

---

court stamps a copy of a will or court pleading as "certified to be a true and correct copy of the original on file with the court" or similar language. Authenticated copies require a triple certification. One certification states that the copies are true and correct copies of the documents on file with the court. Then two other certifications state that the people certifying the documents have authority to act in this capacity. Some states call this an exemplification.

[7] A Proof of Authority is documentation filed with the court showing that a person has been appointed by a court in another state to act on behalf of the estate of a deceased person. Proof of authority does not involve opening a full probate (although the person filing the proof pays the usual court filing fee) and does not involve the issuance of Letters, discussed on page 168. Filing a proof of authority with court gives a personal representative appointed in another state the authority to act in New Mexico. However, if a title company or other business will not accept the Proof of Authority, an ancillary probate proceeding may be required.

[8] Once you reach the Probate Forms page, if you are a WordPerfect user, click on the "File Name" link, starting with 4b. If you are a Microsoft Word user, click on the "TV" (text version) link.

❑ From the New Mexico Rules Annotated, Volume 1, Probate Court Forms.

The applicant is usually the same person as the personal representative. The personal representative must obtain legal authority from the court before acting to settle the decedent's affairs and conduct estate business. After the judge signs the order appointing the personal representative, the court clerk will issue the Letters Testamentary or Letters of Administration discussed above. These Letters are evidence of the personal representative's appointment and authority to act on behalf of the estate.

The do-it-yourself forms contain detailed instructions on how to fill them out.

Checklist for Do-It-Yourself Forms

The following checklist may help *pro se* applicants to complete the do-it-yourself probate forms. In the following list, "you" means "the applicant."

❑ Have you inserted the name of the county where decedent is domiciled in the upper left corner of each form?

❑ Have you correctly spelled the name of decedent and given other names the decedent may be known by?

❑ Have you filled out the form stating your interest in the estate, i.e., your relationship to the decedent?

❑ Are both the date of decedent's death and decedent's age at death stated?

❑ Have you listed the decedent's spouse and all of his/her children, heirs and devisees? The Application must list the decedent's spouse, children, heirs and all devisees (if there is a will), together with their complete address, city, state and zip. Ages of minor children should be listed but no other ages are required. If the personal representative is a spouse, child, heir or devisee of the decedent, then the personal representative should also list himself/herself. For example, if the decedent had no spouse, but had children, you should list the children (and children of any deceased children) and then stops. If the decedent had no spouse or children, then you should list the parents, if any. If no parents, then you should list the next level of heirs, and so on. All devisees (people or entities named as beneficiaries in a will) must also be listed, but not alternate devisees.

❑ If there is a will, is the personal representative who is applying named as first choice? If not, have the proper renunciations/consents been filed?

❑ If there is no will, are there several people who have equal priority? If yes, have they all signed proper renunciations and concurrences? If not, have they at least signed the "I consent to the appointment of the personal representative listed above" section of the do-it-yourself forms? **Note:** if the personal representative with highest priority is not applying to open the probate, then the case must start as a formal proceeding in the district court.

❑ Does the **original** will accompany the Application? If so, you may proceed either in probate or district court. If not, you may only proceed in district court.

❑ Have you called the district court to see if any demands for notice of the probate have been filed with the court about the decedent? Usually, creditors or disgruntled heirs will file this demand so that they receive notice after the probate is opened. Probate courts cannot accept demands for notice until a case is opened. But the district court can accept a demand before a probate is filed. You should check with the district court before filing the initial Application to ask whether any demands for notice have been filed concerning the decedent.

❑ Have 120 hours (5 days) passed since decedent's death? You cannot open a probate until 5 days after death.

❑ Have you signed the Application and the Acceptance of Appointment as Personal Representative in the presence of a notary public? You must state, under oath, that the statements in the Application are true to the best of your knowledge. The Verification must be signed by you in the presence of a notary public, who also signs and notarizes the Verification.

After you have completed the above tasks, you should submit to the court the following:

❑ Notarized Application for Probate
❑ Order for the judge to sign
❑ Notarized Acceptance of Appointment as Personal Representative
❑ Letters Testamentary or Letters of Administration.

The court keeps the originals of these documents for the case file. Submit at least one extra copy of all pleadings, so the court can endorse them and return them to you for your records.

After the court appoints the personal representative, additional paperwork is required. Study the instructions in the forms packet to learn how to proceed.

Priority to Serve as Personal Representative

A personal representative, after appointed by the court, has legal authority to act on behalf of a decedent, settling the estate, paying taxes and creditors and other matters. Personal representatives must be eighteen years of age or older.

New Mexico law sets out who has the highest priority to serve the personal representative. The following list shows who has priority from first to last:

1. Personal representative named in the will;
2. Surviving spouse who is a devisee named in the will;
3. Other devisees of decedent;
4. Surviving spouse of decedent, when there is no will;
5. Other heirs of decedent, when there is no will (if an heir is missing and that missing heir has equal priority to serve as personal representative, only the district court has jurisdiction to appoint);
6. Any interested person, such as a creditor or the state, (other than a spouse, devisee or heir) can apply to have any

qualified person serve. Creditors who ask to be appointed as personal representative must wait **45 days** from decedent's death.

Further, an individual who feloniously and intentionally kills a decedent is barred from serving as personal representative of decedent's estate, even if nominated in decedent's will. An ex-spouse is also barred from serving as personal representative of decedent's estate, even if nominated in decedent's will. One exception would be if a decedent executes a new will **after** the divorce date, naming the ex-spouse as personal representative.

If the personal representative with highest priority does not agree to serve, he or she has two options. First, the personal representative with highest priority can "nominate a qualified person to act as personal representative and thereby confer his relative priority for appointment to his nominee." This means the nominee now has the highest priority to serve. This option does not apply to personal representatives named in a will, but does apply to all others listed above. The do-it-yourself forms do not contain language for this option, so the initial Application form would need to be modified.

Second, a person can "renounce his right to nominate or to appointment by appropriate writing filed with the court. When two or more persons share equal priority, those of them who do not renounce must concur in nominating another to act for them, or in applying for appointment." The do-it-yourself forms contain language about "consenting to the appointment," which others with equal priority to serve as personal representative must sign.

ALL people with equal priority must consent to someone serving as personal representative, and if they will not, they must go to district court in a formal probate proceeding.

Example 1: John dies with a will. He has three children. His will names his surviving spouse Betty as personal representative. The will names his son Bill as the alternate personal representative. Betty declines to serve. Who has priority to serve as personal representative? Bill, because he is the alternate named in the will and first priority to serve are those nominated in the will.

Example 2: Decedent's will names the spouse to serve as personal representative. Spouse is divorced from decedent. Second in line to serve as personal representative in the will is Child A. Who has priority to serve? Child A, since ex-spouses generally lose their right to serve as personal representative and their inheritance rights.

Example 3: Lori is nominated as personal representative in decedent's will. She does not want to serve, so asks her friend Tony to serve on her behalf. Who has priority to serve? Tony does not have priority because, under New Mexico law, a personal representative named in a will cannot confer priority onto another nominee. If a successor personal representative is named in the decedent's will, he or she has next highest priority to serve as personal representative. Otherwise, the surviving spouse (if the spouse is a devisee in the will) has next priority. If there is no spouse, then all devisees named in the will have equal priority to serve as personal representative.

Example 4: Decedent dies without a will. There are four adult children, all living. Who has priority to serve? All four children have equal priority to serve as personal representative. All four must concur in writing to appoint one of them in order for a probate court to have jurisdiction. In the alternative, if none of the children is willing to serve as personal representative, they can all nominate in writing another mutually agreed upon person to serve as personal representative. If they cannot agree on who will serve, the case must be filed in the district court.

Example 5: Decedent dies without a will. There are four adult children, two of whom cannot be found. Who has priority to serve? All four have equal priority. If the other two cannot be found to concur in the appointment of someone, the case must be filed in the district court.

Example 6: Decedent dies without a will. There is no surviving spouse, but there are four adult children, one of whom has died, leaving two adult grandchildren. Who has priority to serve? The three living adult children and two adult grandchildren of the deceased child all have equal priority to serve. All must concur in the appointment of someone as personal representative to use a probate court. If they cannot agree, the case must be filed in the district court.

Example 7: Esperanza is the only child of decedent, who has no will and no spouse. Esperanza is twelve years old. Who has priority to serve? Esperanza must be 18 to serve, but she (or her guardian) can nominate a qualified person to act as personal representative. If this is not done, then other heirs of decedent have equal priority to serve. The next heirs in line to serve are decedent's parents. If both are alive, both have equal priority.

Co-Personal Representatives

Sometimes a will names two individuals to serve as co-personal representatives. They have equal authority to administer the estate, but may delegate tasks between themselves. They must agree on all actions taken on behalf of the estate.

The will may also provide guidance about whether the signatures of both are required in all instances or in selected transactions. For example, a will might state, "Both signatures are required on court paperwork and on transactions involving over $500." It is also possible that people with equal priority to serve as personal representative could concur in two people serving as co-personal representatives.

Successor Personal Representative

Sometimes the personal representative appointed by the court dies, resigns or no longer wishes to serve. Additional paperwork must be submitted to the court asking to have a successor personal representative appointed. If a will exists, hopefully it names a successor personal representative. If no will exists, then the applicant must follow the Priority of Personal Representative rules, discussed above.

Resignation by Personal Representative

A personal representative may resign, but the resignation is **not effective** until a successor personal representative has been appointed and qualified, and the assets delivered to the successor. The personal representative who is resigning has a duty to protect the estate assets and make an accounting to the successor personal representative.

Personal Representative's Bond

The personal representative in some probates may be required to purchase a bond, guaranteed by a surety. A bond provides monetary compensation to beneficiaries and creditors if the personal representative acts improperly in managing the estate.

Most informal probates do not require the personal representative to be bonded, unless the will requires a bond. However, any person whose interest in the estate exceeds $7,500 and any creditor whose claim exceeds $7,500 may make a written demand that a personal representative give bond. The demand must be filed with the court and a copy mailed to the personal representative. The district court will hold a hearing and decide whether to require a bond. If the court requires a bond, the personal representative has **thirty days** to purchase the bond.

Personal Representative's Possible Tasks

❑ Arrange for burial or cremation of decedent.
❑ Locate will, if any, of decedent.
❑ If a probate is necessary, hire an attorney to assist with the probate; sign all necessary court papers.
❑ Complete a change of address form with post office so decedent's mail will forward to the personal representative.
❑ Cancel credit cards to prevent unauthorized charges.
❑ Compile names and current addresses of heirs or devisees.

❑ Get a tax number for the estate,[9] using IRS Form SS-4. The personal representative can also get a tax number on-line at the IRS web site, **www.irs.gov**.

❑ File Estate Federal Income Tax Return, IRS Form 1041, if estate earns more than $600 gross income in a year.

❑ File federal and state income tax forms of the decedent and federal Estate Tax Return, Form 706, if necessary.

❑ Compile a list of decedent's assets and where they are located.

❑ Notify creditors of the decedent's death, compile a list of the decedent's debts, and pay valid creditors' claims.

❑ Notify Social Security and Medicare, if applicable, of decedent's death.

❑ Clean out closets, drawers, garage, sheds, etc. of decedent and hold estate sale if necessary.

❑ Keep an accounting of estate expenses and income.

❑ Distribute the assets of the estate to the heirs or devisees.

Personal Representative's Right to Fees

Personal representatives are entitled to **reasonable** compensation. Personal representatives are also entitled by law to receive from the estate "necessary expenses and disbursements including reasonable attorneys' fees."

Often the personal representative is also an heir and will decline compensation. This is because **fees** awarded to a personal representative are **income**[10] and must be reported on state and federal income tax returns. New Mexico gross receipts tax must also be paid on these fees. To avoid this tax liability, many personal representatives, especially when they will inherit from the estate, choose to waive their fee. If so, a written renunciation of the fee may be filed with the court.

---

[9]This number is called an Employer Identification Number (EIN), but is also used for trusts and estates.

[10]This also applies to trustee's fees.

Inheritances, on the other hand, are specifically excluded from the IRS's definition of income and do not generally trigger income tax liability. Heirs and devisees usually do not report inheritances on federal or state income tax returns, unless the inheritance is "income in respect of a decedent," discussed on page 109.

Calculating a fair fee depends on the work you are doing for the estate. For instance, if you are clearing out a garage, a fee of $10 or $15 an hour, not $50 an hour, is probably reasonable. If you are filing taxes, meeting with professionals, or preparing accountings, then a higher hourly rate might be charged.

To give some perspective, earning $20 an hour for a full-time job would yield about $40,000 a year; $50 an hour would be over $100,000. Personal representatives do not normally work full-time to settle an estate, so their fees should be much less than a full-time salary.

Fees will vary from estate to estate. Much depends on the amount of time spent, the complexity of the tasks, the degree of skill necessary, the size of the estate and other criteria. If you are a CPA, tax attorney or other professional with special expertise, charging your regular professional rate for certain services may be reasonable. (Banks and financial companies generally charge 1 to 1.5% of the estate assets per year as fees to manage property such as trusts, and more if special circumstances are involved.)

There are no hard and fast rules for calculating compensation. But the law allows "any interested person" to ask the court to review the reasonableness of compensation of personal representatives, as well as fees paid to professionals hired on behalf of the estate. The court may order any person who has received excessive compensation to make appropriate refunds to the estate.

Keeping a detailed log of the date, time spent, and tasks accomplished should help personal representatives to justify their fees. Discussing proposed fees with those who are receiving estate assets may avoid future disputes.

Special Administrators

Sometimes someone will need to start a probate before all renunciations or other paperwork are complete. The probate and district courts have jurisdiction to appoint special administrators to act on behalf of an estate before a regular personal representative is appointed. The special administrator has the duty to collect and manage the estate assets, to preserve them, and to account for and deliver the assets to the personal representative after the personal representative is appointed. The do-it-yourself probate forms do not contain language for requesting a special administrator and would need to be modified.

If the applicant started with an Application for Appointment of Special Administrator, the applicant can use that same case file to convert the case to a regular probate case. The court would appoint a personal representative after the applicant requested it. Usually, a separate case number and second docket fee are not required.

Who are the Decedent's Heirs?

Knowing who the heirs are is important because New Mexico law requires the heirs of an estate to be listed in the Application even if the heir is omitted from a will or specifically disinherited.

Personal representatives of the estate are also required to give the decedent's spouse, children, heirs and devisees **notice** of their appointment within ten days of their appointment. This is required so that heirs are informed about the probate and have an opportunity to challenge the will or appointment of personal representative. If a will were proved to be invalid, the heirs would inherit the estate.

For example, suppose Mom's will leaves her estate to three of her four children, but omits the fourth child. If a court probate proceeding is necessary, the fourth child must be listed in the initial Application for probate and given notice of the appointment of a personal representative within ten days of the appointment. This notice gives the omitted child an opportunity to challenge the will and also protects the personal representative, who must follow

Mom's wishes expressed in her will in distributing assets.

The first heirs are decedent's spouse and children, both by blood and adoption. If one or more of decedent's children have died, all children of the deceased child or children are also considered heirs of the decedent's estate and must be listed.

If the decedent had neither a spouse nor children, decedent's parents are the heirs, if both survive, or the surviving parent.

If the decedent has no surviving spouse, children or parents, then decedent's brothers and sisters are the heirs; (if one or more of decedent's siblings has died, the children of the deceased sibling(s) are also heirs of the estate).

If the decedent has no surviving spouse, children, parents or siblings, the decedent's grandparents are the heirs—if the grandparents are deceased, their children (decedent's aunts and uncles), are the heirs of the estate.

If there are also no aunts or uncles (or children of aunts and uncles) then more distant relatives are the heirs of the estate.

If no relatives of the decedent can be found, the estate "escheats" to the state school fund.

If the applicant does not know who or where some of the heirs are, he or she has a duty to perform a reasonably diligent search for them. In New Mexico, any heir who fails to survive a decedent by 120 hours (5 days) is deemed to have died before the decedent.

Important Notes: An individual who feloniously and intentionally kills a decedent is barred from inheriting decedent's estate, even if included in decedent's will. An ex-spouse is also barred from inheriting decedent's estate, unless a court order or contract states otherwise. **Exception**: a decedent could execute a new will **after** the divorce date, including the ex-spouse as a devisee. A spouse from whom the decedent was separated, but not yet divorced still has inheritance rights.

A child may inherit from the estate of a parent who refused to support them, but a parent who has refused to support a child cannot inherit from the estate of that deceased child.

What if a Personal Representative is Acting Badly?

If a case began in the probate court and the personal representative is mismanaging the estate, an interested person may seek the removal of the personal representative or the supervised administration discussed above. This proceeding must be brought in the district court, which would require the filing of a new case, along with paying a new filing fee.

If the case started in the district court, interested people can file petitions for removal in the existing probate case and request a hearing by the judge on removing or supervising the personal representative.

The law allows any interested person to petition to remove a personal representative for cause at any time. Cause for removal exists when the personal representative: (1) misrepresented material facts that led to the appointment; (2) disregarded a court order; (3) is incapable of performing his or her duties; (4) mismanaged the estate; or (5) failed to perform any duty of office, including failure to provide inventories and accountings to interested persons. The court can also find that removal is in the best interests of the estate.

The district court sets a time and place for a hearing, listens to all of the evidence, and decides whether to remove the personal representative. After the personal representative receives notice of the hearing, he or she shall not act except to account, correct maladministration, or preserve the estate, pending further instructions from the court.

Personal representatives may avoid disputes by openly and honestly communicating with beneficiaries and by promptly providing copies of estate documents, as required by law or upon request. Families may choose first to attempt a more informal mediation before starting a court proceeding for removal.

Real Property as Part of Estate

Estates involving real property (such as land, houses, farms, ranches, gas and mineral rights) may require additional court procedures in order to pass clear title on to the heirs or devisees.

The general rule is that transfer of title to real property must be recorded in the clerk's office of the county of the state where each piece of real property is located.

The personal representative appointed by the court has legal authority to sell real property or to transfer title to it via a "Personal Representative's Deed" from the estate to the new owner(s). Having an attorney prepare this deed is important so that title is properly passed to the new owners. The new owners should then change the names on the property tax assessment records and acquire homeowner's insurance, if applicable, in their own name.

The Personal Representative's Deed must be signed by the personal representative in the presence of a notary public who notarizes the deed. The Personal Representative's Deed must be recorded in the county clerk's office in the county where the real property is located. A **certified**[11] copy of the deed may also be included in the probate case file. Recording the death certificate of the decedent in every county where the real property is located is also wise.

The will may state that the real property is to be sold rather than transferred to the heirs. In this case the personal representative will sell the real property (completing a Personal Representative's Deed to the new owners) and divide the proceeds among the beneficiaries, according to the terms of the will, if any, or laws of intestate succession.

The real property may have to be sold in order to pay creditors of the estate. To avoid future problems, the personal representative's attorney often writes the heirs before selling the property, telling them the proposed purchase price and asking for their approval. This communication is not required, but can prevent future complaints by the heirs.

Depending on the terms of a decedent's will, the personal

[11]See footnote 2.

representative may use, sell or restrict the use of a property's natural resources, such as timber or minerals lying beneath the surface. However, other natural resources, such as surface and underground water, oil and gas, move about without regard to property lines. Their removal is subject to state and federal regulations. The personal representative passing title to such property should consult an attorney about these matters.

One other thing to consider if real property is part of the estate is whether the surviving spouse is eligible to continue a decedent's veteran's property tax exemption. If the decedent had an exemption, it needs to be transferred to the surviving spouse. The Veteran's Administration requires certain paperwork, including: (1) the original copy of the veteran's property tax exemption, (2) an original death certificate for the veteran, and (3) proof of domicile of the surviving spouse, such as voter's registration or a copy of a New Mexico income tax return. With the proper paperwork, the spouse can keep benefiting from this exemption. Contact your local Veteran's Administration office for information.

Probate Opened in One County, Real Property Located in Another New Mexico County

A decedent may own property in a New Mexico county **other than** the usual place of residence. If so, New Mexico law requires a **Notice of Administration** to be recorded with the County Clerk in each New Mexico county (other than the county where the probate is opened) where the decedent owns real property. The New Mexico law states that if real property is included in an estate and is in a county other than the county where the estate is being administered, the personal representative shall (or any other interested person may) record with the county clerk of the other county a notice of administration setting forth:

(1) the name of the decedent;

(2) the title and docket number of the administration proceedings;

(3) a description of the type of administration;

(4) the court wherein instituted;

(5) the name, address and title of the personal representative; and

(6) a complete description of the real property situate in such county.

Real Property Located Outside of New Mexico

If a decedent owned real property outside the state where the decedent was domiciled at death, additional procedures to pass clear title to the property may be necessary in the other state where the property is located. If a probate was **first** opened in the state of decedent's domicile at death, then an **ancillary proceeding** could occur in the state where the real property was located.

This situation could arise under two circumstances: 1) decedent died domiciled in New Mexico, but owned real estate, oil, gas or other mineral rights, in another location outside of New Mexico; or 2) decedent died domiciled outside of New Mexico, but owned real estate, oil, gas or other mineral rights within New Mexico.

In the first circumstance, an ancillary probate or other proceeding could be required in the other state, depending on that state's law. In the second circumstance, the personal representative would open an ancillary probate in New Mexico if a probate had already been opened in the state of domicile.

If a probate had **not** been opened in the state of domicile in the second circumstance, one could open an original probate in New Mexico. This would not be an ancillary proceeding, however.

If a probate has already been opened in the state of domicile, New Mexico law allows an informal probate of a will that has been previously probated in another state or foreign country to be granted at any time upon written application by any interested person, together with an authenticated copy of the will and of the order or statement probating it from the office or court where it was first probated.

For **intestate** cases where the decedent is not domiciled in New Mexico, if a probate has been opened in the state of domicile, an applicant who is the domiciliary personal representative (the person appointed in the place the decedent was domiciled) may open an informal probate proceeding in New Mexico.

New Mexico law also allows formal ancillary proceedings in a district court.

The personal representative should contact the court and/or the county clerk's office in the state where the property is located for more information on how to proceed. Searching on the Internet for various state's laws and court procedures can provide some of this information.

Manufactured (Mobile) Homes as Part of Estate

Some people think that manufactured (mobile) homes are real property. Since most manufactured homes are moveable, they are considered personal property like automobiles and must be registered and licensed. They usually have license plates like vehicles. Unless they are permanently affixed to the ground, manufactured homes receive a title from the Motor Vehicles Division (MVD).

Often, if a manufactured home is titled in the sole name of the decedent, MVD will allow the personal representative to transfer title through a form, called "Certificate of Transfer Without Probate." This Certificate is similar to an "Affidavit of Successor in Interest," discussed on page 203. Check MVD's web site, **http://www.state.nm.us/tax/mvd/mvd_home.htm**, for more information.

Paying Family and Personal Property Allowances

As discussed in Chapter Four, New Mexico law allots $30,000 of decedent's estate to a surviving spouse as a **family allowance**. If a decedent has no surviving spouse, then decedent's minor and dependent children share the $30,000 in equal shares. This family allowance is exempt from and has priority over all claims against the estate, including creditors' claims.

New Mexico also allows a $15,000 **personal property**

allowance to decedent's surviving spouse. If a decedent has no surviving spouse, then decedent's children, except those intentionally omitted from decedent's will, receive the allowance. This personal property allowance is exempt from and has priority over all claims against the estate, except for the family allowance.

It is the personal representative's responsibility to see that the allowances owed, if any, are paid to the correct recipients.

Paying Debts of Decedent

The personal representative is responsible for paying the debts of the decedent. These debts might include burial expenses, medical bills, credit card debts, mortgage payments or other obligations.

If assets of the estate are insufficient to pay all claims in full, New Mexico law requires the personal representative to pay claims in the following order, from highest to lowest priority:

1st costs and expenses of administration, including compensation of personal representatives and persons employed by the personal representatives, such as attorneys, accountants, appraisers and others;

2nd reasonable funeral expenses;

3rd debts and taxes with preference under federal law;

4th reasonable medical and hospital expenses of decedent's last illness, including compensation of persons attending the decedent;

5th debts and taxes with preference under other laws of New Mexico; and

6th all other unsecured claims, such as utility and credit card bills.

The personal representative must pay claims in the order of priority listed, after making provisions for family and personal property allowances, if applicable.

The personal representative should not give preference to paying one claim over any other claim of the same class. To the extent that funds are not available to pay all claims within one class in full, the creditor is entitled to receive payment of an equal proportion of his claim.

Generally, personal representatives who act in good faith as fiduciaries for the estate are not individually liable for decedent's debts. But a personal representative can be personally liable if he or she pays a lower priority creditor instead of a higher priority creditor. A personal representative may also be personally liable for payment of estate taxes.

Important Law About Life Insurance Proceeds. New Mexico law provides that the "proceeds of any life insurance are not subject to the debts of the decedent, except by special contract or arrangement made in writing." This means that even if the decedent owed money for medical bills, funeral expenses, business loans and other debts, the life insurance paid to beneficiaries **could not** be attached by creditors to pay those debts.[12]

Paying Creditors' Claims from Other Assets of Decedent

Creditors can also recover funds needed to pay claims from property that passes outside of probate, such as payable on death accounts and joint tenancy property. If the probate estate of decedent is insufficient to pay the debts, creditors can reach payable on death (POD) and transfer on death (TOD) property that has already been distributed outside of a probate proceeding.

"If other assets of the estate are insufficient," the law reads, "a transfer resulting from a right of survivorship or POD designation…is not effective against the estate of a deceased party to the extent needed to pay claims against the estate and statutory allowances to the surviving spouse and children." The law governing transfer on death deeds (TODDs) for real property contains virtually identical language.

The law sets out the procedure for recovering joint tenancy and POD funds. The recipient beneficiary is liable to account to the

---

[12]The family allowance and personal property allowances are also exempt from creditors' claims.

decedent's personal representative. The personal representative has the power to commence a proceeding to recover the funds after he or she receives a written demand for payment from a surviving spouse, child or creditor of the decedent. This proceeding must be started within one year after decedent's death.

Under a different section of the law, a personal representative can stop a financial institution from paying the beneficiary by sending a written notice of a pending dispute to the institution. The financial institution can then refuse, without liability, to make payment to the beneficiary.

The TOD laws for stocks and security accounts also considers creditors' rights. The TOD laws do "not limit the rights of creditors of security owners against beneficiaries and other transferees under other laws of this state."

Creditors can now also reach trust property under the Uniform Trust Act (UTC), discussed in Chapter Five. The UTC states that the property of a revocable trust is subject to the claims of the settlor's creditors, costs of administration of the settlor's estate, funeral expenses and statutory allowances to a surviving spouse and children. This provision applies if the settlor's probate estate is inadequate to satisfy those claims, costs, expenses and allowances.

If there is any possibility of problems among the beneficiaries, probating the assets rather than using all POD, TOD or joint beneficiary designations to pass assets may be more efficient and economical. Having the assets in hand to pay bills, taxes, etc. and then distributing the rest is easier than collecting assets back from reluctant beneficiaries. If the beneficiaries have spent the money, recovering it could prove difficult.

As long as family members are reasonable, a court procedure should not be necessary.

Insufficient Assets to Pay All of Decedent's Debts

If the decedent's total assets are insufficient to pay all claims, creditors with a lower priority claim are out of luck. For example, Juan, who is divorced, dies leaving an eight-year-old son. Juan's total assets are $60,000. Costs and expenses of administration are $2,000. Funeral costs are $5,500. Federal taxes are $1,500. Hospital expenses not covered by insurance or Medicare are $30,000. No state taxes are due. Credit card debts total $10,000.

Juan's minor son receives the first $45,000 to satisfy the family and personal property allowances. A conservator will manage the $45,000 until the son reaches the age of majority. The personal representative should then pay the first three claims totaling $9,000. This leaves only $6,000 toward the hospital bills. Twenty percent of each hospital bill will be paid. The credit card companies receive nothing and will have to "write off" the debt.

Tax Considerations of Probate

As mentioned above, gifts and inheritances are **not** usually considered gross income by the IRS and are **not** usually subject to income tax. Federal law authorizes the IRS to collect **estate tax** on certain estates. Estate tax is different from **income tax**.

Generally, estates with a taxable value of $1,500,000 (in 2004 and 2005) or less owe no estate taxes, federal or New Mexico, when a person dies. Estate taxes and how to calculate the fair market value of an estate are discussed on page 148.

The personal representative is also responsible for filing any state or federal **income tax returns** for the decedent. Income tax returns for the estate would be required if the estate assets earned more than $600 gross income in a year. As mentioned previously, the personal representative would file an income tax Form 1041 for the estate and use the special tax I.D. number for the estate (*see* page 182). Using the tax number for the estate, rather than the personal representative's social security number, will prevent estate income from being charged personally to the personal representative. IRS Publication 559 for Survivors, Executors, and Administrators contains helpful information about these tax topics.

One interesting Internal Revenue Code section relates to gifts made during a person's lifetime. For example, X adds Y's name to her home as a joint tenant. Y does not pay X for any of the property. X dies. As discussed above, the property is valued as of the date of X's death. Normally, only half of the property is considered part of X's estate because Y is a joint tenant. But the IRS instead considers the entire value of the property to be included in X's gross estate. This means the entire value of property receives a **stepped-up basis**.

Distributing Assets to Beneficiaries

Personal representatives generally do not distribute assets until the time for filing creditor claims has expired. The personal representative must pay valid creditor claims, pay decedent's federal and state income and estate taxes, pay the New Mexico family and personal property allowances due (if any), prepare an accounting, and distribute the estate assets properly. The personal representative must follow the provisions of the will, if any, or intestate laws, if no will exists.

The personal representative should not distribute any assets until after completing the inventory and appraisal of the assets of the estate. If the estate is large and the debts are few, the personal representative may make a **partial distribution** to the beneficiaries of some of the assets in the estate. Because the personal representative is acting on behalf of the estate and not on behalf of the beneficiaries, being fair and impartial is important. The personal representative should make partial distributions to the beneficiaries in equal shares and reserve sufficient funds to pay creditors.

The personal representative must distribute all of the assets before closing the estate. After the estate is closed, the personal representative no longer has legal authority to act for the estate.

An important point: After beneficiaries receive the assets from the estate of a decedent, the beneficiaries own the assets. Often a will states, "I give my property to X, but if X does not survive me, then to Y." The maker of the will dies. X inherits the property. X dies. Y then calls an attorney and asks for help in obtaining the property because Y thinks that because X has died, Y is now entitled to receive the property. Y is wrong. After the property passes to X, X owns the property. X's will controls who next inherits the property. The only way Y would inherit the property would be if X died **before the maker of the will died.**

Agreements Among Successors

Despite the principle that the intent of the testator is all-important, New Mexico law allows successors to an estate to change the testator's wishes. The heirs or devisees may unanimously agree among themselves to alter the interests, shares or amounts to which they are entitled under the will or laws of intestate succession. This agreement is subject to the rights of creditors and taxing authorities.

All of the people whose interests are affected must sign a written agreement in order to alter an inheritance. Although the law does not say so, a copy of this written agreement should be filed in the court file. Otherwise, problems could arise later if a dispute occurred over the distribution of the property.

Disclaiming an Inheritance

Disclaimers are used when someone who is supposed to receive decedent's property does not want it (for tax or other reasons). Disclaimers must comply with federal Internal Revenue Code requirements and New Mexico law.[13]

Qualified disclaimers under federal tax law must be in writing and made within nine months of decedent's death. The person making the disclaimer cannot use or benefit from the disclaimed property.

New Mexico's law on disclaimers contains no time limit. The law was amended in 2001 to allow a disclaimer to be:

❑ delivered to the personal representative of the decedent's estate; or

---

[13]New Mexico's law on disclaimers appears in the New Mexico Statutes Annotated, Sections 46-10-1 through 46-10-17.

❑ if no personal representative is serving, it must be filed with a court having jurisdiction to appoint the personal representative.

Under these provisions, someone could open a case in probate or district court for the sole purpose of filing a disclaimer. The court docket fee would still be paid and the case would be docketed as if it were a regular probate case. No further filings relating to the disclaimer appear to be required.

Summary Administration for Very Small Estates

In very small estates, if the value of the entire estate, less liens and encumbrances, does not exceed the family allowance, personal property allowance, cost and expenses of administration, decedent's reasonable and necessary medical and hospital expenses, and reasonable funeral expenses, the law allows the personal representative to immediately distribute the estate assets without giving notice to creditors. This is called a **summary administration.**

In a summary administration, the personal representative files a closing statement that states the following:

1) to the best of their knowledge, the value of the entire estate, less liens and encumbrances, did not exceed:

❑ the family allowance;
❑ personal property allowance;
❑ costs and expenses of administration;
❑ reasonable and necessary medical and hospital expenses of last illness of the decedent; and
❑ reasonable funeral expenses.

2) the personal representative has fully administered the estate by disbursing and distributing it to the persons entitled thereto; and

3) the personal representative has sent a copy of the closing statement to all distributees of the estate and to all creditors or other claimants of whom he is aware whose claims are neither paid nor barred; and,

4) the personal representative has furnished a full account in

writing of his administration to all distributees whose interests are affected.

If no proceedings involving the personal representative are pending in district court one year after the verified statement (or statement of summary administration) is filed, the appointment of the personal representative terminates.

Closing a Probate—Three Ways

After the personal representative has performed all duties required under the probate code and done everything necessary to administer the estate, the personal representative can close the estate in one of three ways.

Closing formally: When real property is part of the estate, many attorneys close a probate **formally**.[14] This involves filing a **Petition to Close** along with a **Final Accounting.** Many attorneys also give a **Schedule of Distribution of the Assets** to interested persons and the court. These documents are sent to the heirs, devisees and others prior to the court hearing. If the probate is closed formally, the court will schedule a short hearing, and the personal representative or attorney will send **notice** of the hearing to all heirs, devisees and other interested people, as well as publish notice to unknown heirs. The judge will hold a short hearing before approving the distribution of the assets to the heirs or devisees. The judge will sign an **Order for Complete Distribution of the Estate** to close the probate of the estate. Anyone who is unhappy with the outcome of the probate or distribution of assets has **thirty days** after the judge signs the order to appeal to the New Mexico Court of Appeals in Santa Fe. This thirty-day time limit does not usually apply to a missing heir who never knew about the original probate proceeding. Closing formally means that after thirty days the personal representative is no longer liable for the estate, unless the personal representative defrauded the estate.

---

[14]Remember that an estate can only be closed formally in district court. An estate cannot be closed formally in probate court.

Closing informally: If the probate is closed **informally,**[15] the judge will not hold a hearing. After distributing the assets of the estate, the personal representative may file with the court a **Verified Closing Statement** that says the estate is fully administered and distributed. State law says this statement can be done "**no earlier than three months** after the date of original appointment of a general personal representative for the estate." The do-it-yourself probate forms include a Verified Closing Statement.

A personal representative must send a copy of the closing statement to all distributees of the estate and to all creditors and other claimants of whom the personal representative is aware. A personal representative must also furnish a full account in writing of the administration of the estate to those distributees whose interests are affected.

The personal representative should send copies of the closing statement to the beneficiaries of the estate. The judge does **not** sign an order closing the estate.

If the personal representative breached his or her duty while serving, there is some relief after the closing statement is filed. The law says that claims of creditors (whose claims are not otherwise barred) and successors against the personal representative are barred unless commenced within **six months** after the filing of the closing statement. This six-month rule does not apply to actions to recover from a personal representative for fraud, misrepresentation or inadequate disclosure related to settling the decedent's estate.

The Verified Statement must be signed by the personal representative under oath in the presence of a notary public. If no proceedings involving the personal representative are pending in the district court **one year** after the verified statement is filed, the **appointment** of the personal representative terminates.

Not Closing at All: New Mexico law does not **require** a probate to be closed. Sometimes a personal representative will

---

[15] An estate can be closed informally in probate court or district court.

distribute the assets of the estate to the beneficiaries without giving notice to anyone and without a court order. This might occur if the probate is routine and the personal representative anticipates no challenges to the probate.

Creditors' claims are barred one year after the decedent's death. Those who receive the assets can be liable for other claims against the estate for three years after the decedent's death or one year after the asset was distributed, whichever is later. These same time periods apply to a personal representative's liability if the estate is not closed at all. On the other hand, some personal representatives want official termination of their duties by the court and opt for an informal or formal closing.

Sometimes a person will be killed in an automobile or work-related accident. The estate will want to sue the person or company at fault. New Mexico law includes a section called the Wrongful Death Act (WDA). In order for a personal representative to proceed under the WDA, a probate may be opened informally in probate or district court solely to appoint a personal representative. If a personal representative is appointed in a probate proceeding, he or she is subject to all requirements of the probate code, as well as the WDA. A representative can also be appointed as part of the WDA action in district court without opening a separate probate case. Once appointed, a personal representative will pursue the wrongful death claim under the WDA on the decedent's behalf. If the proceeds from a wrongful death lawsuit are the only asset of the estate, distribution of these assets will be governed by the WDA, not the probate code. The probate proceeding will usually not be closed.

Optional Certificate of the Court

The personal representative of the estate may submit an Application for Certificate of the Court at any time after filing the Verified Statement or Statement of Summary Administration. A Certificate of Full Administration releases any liens on property posted by the personal representative in lieu of bond, but does not preclude any action against the personal representative. Judges cannot sign the Certificate of the Court until one year has passed since the Verified Statement was filed.

In reality, this is more of a formality, since bond is usually not required of the personal representative in the probate court. The case is considered closed whether the court issues the order or not. But some people feel better if they have an actual order closing the case.

Newly Discovered Property

On occasion, years after a probate case is closed, someone will discover that decedent owned other property that was not included as part of the original probate. If it has been more than one year since the verified closing statement has been filed, the case will have to be reopened in the district court. If this other property is discovered after an estate is settled and the personal representative discharged, only the district court has jurisdiction to appoint a successor personal representative to administer the subsequently discovered property.

Reopening Old Cases for Mistake or Inadvertence

A different scenario might occur if property was included in decedent's original probate, but for some reason, proper title was not transferred or another mistake occurred. In that instance, an applicant can ask the court to reopen the old case and reappoint a former personal representative or appoint a successor personal representative to fix the mistake. Additional paperwork must be submitted to the court.

Example 1: Mr. Z died in 1971. He had a valid will. A probate was properly opened in the probate court. An inventory of Mr. Z's property was prepared and filed with the court. The personal representative failed to complete a personal representative's deed for one lot listed on the inventory. The estate was closed. Thirty years later, when the property is about to be sold, the title company discovers that clear title was never passed to the lot. In which court can this case be reopened? In the probate court, if additional court paperwork is submitted. If the former personal representative is deceased, the court should look at the will to determine who is next in line to serve. After appointed by the court, the personal representative will have legal authority to complete the personal representative's deed and clear the title to the lot.

Example 2: Ms. X died in 1981. A probate was properly opened in the probate court. An inventory of Ms. X's property was prepared and filed with the court, but failed to include Lot 47, which the personal representative did not know about. The estate was closed. Twenty years later, when the property is about to be sold, the title company discovers that clear title was never passed to Lot 47. In which court can this case be reopened? Lot 47 is "newly discovered property" and the case must be filed in district court. (This same scenario could also apply to personal property such as newly discovered stocks, bonds or bank accounts.)

Example 3: Ms. Y died in 1991 without a will. A probate was properly opened in the probate court. No inventory was filed with the court. The estate was never officially closed. Eleven years later, a certificate of deposit is discovered at a local bank. In which court can this case be continued? Because the case was never closed, the personal representative, if still living, continues to have authority to act. If a successor personal representative is needed, additional paperwork must be filed. The probate court will issue certified Letters of Administration showing the personal representative still has authority to act.

Costs of Probate

If a personal representative is filing a probate *pro se*, the applicant will pay the court filing fee and fee to publish notice to creditors. If the personal representative is using an attorney, he or she will also have to pay attorney's fees. The attorney should discuss the fee arrangement with the personal representative before beginning the case. Many attorneys prepare written fee agreements so that the terms of payment are clear.

Attorneys, personal representatives and others doing business on behalf of the estate may charge **reasonable** fees. All interested persons have the right to challenge the reasonableness of fees in court. If the court finds that any person has received excessive compensation, the person may be ordered to make appropriate refunds to the estate.

Attorneys' hourly rates vary, as does the amount of time spent on a particular probate. A routine, uncontested probate with assets such as a home, bank accounts and stocks should generally take the attorney five to twenty hours to complete. This time estimate may vary depending on how much work the personal representative does or whether the probate attorney is involved in the sale of real estate.

Transferring Assets Without a Probate

There are several ways to transfer assets without going through the probate proceeding in court. Chapter Four discusses **joint tenancy** in detail. **POD accounts, TOD accounts, TODDs** and assets with named **beneficiaries** pass outside of probate. Property held in **trusts** or **trust accounts** does not have to go through probate to pass to the beneficiaries. New Mexico law provides several others ways to avoid probate.

Affidavit of successor in interest. An affidavit is a sworn, notarized statement. The affidavit of successor in interest can be used without a court proceeding to collect small amounts of a decedent's personal property under certain conditions. The person or persons entitled to receive a decedent's property through this affidavit are called **successors in interest**. If more than one person is entitled to receive a decedent's property, all successors must sign the affidavit.

The successors can sign an affidavit of successor in interest if: (1) the total amount of the person's estate that needs to be probated is less than $30,000; (2) thirty days have passed since the person died; and (3) no one has applied as personal representative of the estate. A sample affidavit appears in Appendix 2—Forms, Form 5.

This law applies to bank accounts, stocks, bonds, vehicles, mobile homes and other personal property, but **not** to land, houses or other real property. If the decedent had other property that passed outside of probate through joint tenancy, POD or TOD accounts, one could still use this affidavit if the assets subject to probate did not exceed $30,000.

The successors in interest would be those named in a will or the intestate heirs if the decedent had no will. The successors to the personal property would sign the affidavit in the presence of a notary public and present the affidavit to the individual, corporation, bank or agency holding the property owned by the decedent.

This affidavit is most often used to collect funds held in a decedent's bank account and to have the title to a decedent's motor vehicle or mobile home transferred to the successors. The New Mexico Motor Vehicle Division has its own affidavit form for successors to sign. Other kinds of personal property owned by a decedent, such as stocks or bonds, can be collected with this affidavit.

Sometimes businesses will balk at accepting these affidavits. If the personal property to be collected by the successors is located outside New Mexico, an out-of-state corporation might be even more reluctant to transfer ownership of the assets to the successors using an affidavit. New Mexico law protects companies that rely on the affidavit by relieving them of liability if they transfer property through an affidavit. If the affidavit is refused, however, a simple probate proceeding should allow a personal representative to transfer the assets.

Transfer of homestead by affidavit. This procedure will help only **husbands** and **wives** who do not have a joint tenancy deed to their home. Sometimes a husband and wife will own their home as community property (this means they bought the home during the marriage), but the deed to the home does not say "joint tenants." Normally, if this were the case, the surviving spouse would have to go through probate to transfer the home into his or her name. New

Mexico has a special law that states when one spouse dies, if there is no will or if the deceased spouse's will gave an interest in the home to the surviving spouse, then the home transfers automatically without going through probate.

To use this special affidavit, (1) the home must be community property; (2) the assessed value of the home for property tax purposes cannot exceed $100,000; (3) the only asset of the decedent's probate estate must be his or her one-half interest in the home and, except for the home, there is no reason for a probate proceeding either in district court or probate court; and (4) the home involved must be the principal place of residence of the decedent or surviving spouse or the last principal place of residence. If these requirements are met, clear legal title to the home passes to the surviving spouse **without a probate.**

In order to use this affidavit, six months must have passed since the first spouse's death. The surviving spouse must file an affidavit (sworn and notarized statement), along with a certified death certificate for the deceased spouse, with the county clerk to record the transfer. The affidavit should state that: (1) six months have elapsed since the spouse's death; (2) the surviving spouse and deceased spouse were married at the time of death and owned the home as community property; (3) a copy of the old deed to the home is attached to the affidavit; (4) except for the home, no probate of the decedent's estate is necessary; (5) no one has applied to be personal representative or started a probate proceeding in court; (6) all funeral expenses and other debts have been paid; (7) the affiant (spouse who signs the affidavit) is the surviving spouse and is entitled to the title to the home; (8) no one else has a right to the property; (9) no federal or state taxes are due; and (10) the statements in the affidavit are true and correct. If you are unsure about how to prepare and file this affidavit, using an attorney is recommended. A sample affidavit appears in Appendix 2—Forms, Form 6.

Employee paycheck provision. New Mexico law allows the surviving **spouse** of a deceased person, without starting a probate procedure, to collect any final paychecks owed to the decedent for wages, earnings, salary, commission, travel or other reimbursement. The spouse would need to present an affidavit (sworn and notarized statement) to obtain release of these monies.

Bank/Credit Union Accounts of $2,000 or Less. New Mexico law also allows financial institutions or credit unions to release a decedent's funds of $2,000 or less to a surviving spouse or next of kin legally entitled to the funds. The person claiming the money does not have to sign an Affidavit of Successor in Interest or start a probate. The bank or credit union will probably ask to see a copy of the death certificate and may ask to see a copy of the will before releasing the funds. The law allows the banks and credit unions to use their discretion in turning over these funds; they are not **required** to do so.

Life Estate. Some people who own a house will set up a life estate. This means the person, called a **life tenant**, can live in the house during his or her lifetime. When the life tenant dies, the house would pass to the named **remaindermen** (people who are named in the deed to receive the property after the life tenant dies) without a probate proceeding. The new owners would need to record the death certificate at the county clerk's office in the county where the house is located. Setting up a life estate requires a new deed to the house to be prepared, signed, notarized and recorded in the county where the house is located.

Setting up a life estate may create problems. The life tenant loses control over the property. The life tenant does not actually own the property anymore but is only allowed to live there. The life tenant may not sell the property, except for the value of the life estate (someone could buy the property and live in it only during the owner's lifetime). The life tenant must pay all taxes, insurance, upkeep and repairs. The life tenant and new owners may not agree on what kind of upkeep needs to be done. The life tenant may be ineligible for nursing home benefits, discussed in Chapter Three, because the Human Services Department considers a life estate as a resource with value. Finally, if the original owner creates a life estate, the heirs will not receive a stepped-up basis for the property when the original owner dies (see page 158 for definition of stepped-up basis). If the house had passed instead through a probate proceeding or through a trust, the heirs would receive the stepped-up basis and not owe any capital gains tax if they sold the house.

Personal Property Only. In many cases, all of the assets of the deceased person have passed through joint tenancy, POD accounts, TOD accounts or otherwise without needing a probate proceeding. If only personal effects remain, the family can divide the estate informally among themselves unless there is a dispute about the items. It is rarely worth the expense and time of going to court to resolve disputes over items of personal property.

Problems to Attempt to Avoid in Probate

Invalid wills are a frustrating problem for heirs, devisees and lawyers. A person may have created a will specifying who should receive property, but the will is not properly signed or dated or witnessed. The court would probably not accept this will and would proceed as if the deceased person had no will. The New Mexico laws of **intestate succession** (discussed in Chapter Four) set out who inherits property if no valid will exists.

Missing heirs can be a problem if someone dies without a valid will. The personal representative would have to search for the missing heirs even if they had not been heard from in many years. If a person has a valid will that leaves assets to people who cannot be found, the personal representative will also have to search for the heirs. After a diligent search, if the heir has been missing for five years, the district court can declare the heir legally dead.

Contested probates can take many years, cause many arguments among family members and cost many dollars to resolve. While there is always a chance that a will can be contested or challenged, having a valid will makes it much harder to do so. It is recommended that an attorney help prepare a will. A person should also keep current, detailed records about all business and financial affairs, as well as a current address book of friends and relatives.

Probates in several states can trigger additional paperwork, requirements, time delays and expenses. Different states have different procedures, plus attorneys are only allowed to practice law in states in which they are licensed. If you need to open probate cases in several states, you will probably need to hire several attorneys to help you. A properly drafted and funded living trust should avoid this problem.

Simultaneous Deaths

People often ask what happens if they die simultaneously in an automobile accident or other accident. In reality, this rarely happens. New Mexico law does require that heirs survive the decedent by one hundred and twenty hours. If a simultaneous death occurs, the person is deemed to have predeceased the other and the decedent's heirs are determined accordingly. Unless a will sets out specific simultaneous death or other related provisions, "one-half of the property passes as if one had survived by 120 hours and one-half as if the other had survived by 120 hours." This probably means one-half of the property passes to the heirs of each of the deceased. Two probates usually occur in instances of simultaneous death.

Start Probate Within Three Years After Death

New Mexico law states the general rule that a probate cannot be started more than three years after the decedent's death. If three years have passed, **even if** the decedent left a will, the will does not control. A few exceptions to this general rule exist, including one that allows an informal appointment of personal representative more than three years after decedent's death for the sole purpose of confirming title to the appropriate successors. The personal representative has no right to possess estate assets other than to confirm title. Creditors claims, other than expenses of administration, may not be presented against the estate at this late date.

If decedent had a will, New Mexico law appears to require a formal testacy proceeding. Only the district court would have jurisdiction in this circumstance.

A formal probate proceeding may be started after the three-year period "for the purpose of establishing an instrument to direct or control the ownership of property" to preserve clear title when other possible owners are involved.

In other instances, the court might conduct a **determination of heirship** procedure or a **quiet title** suit if real property is involved. A quiet title suit is a court proceeding to determine the legal owner of a piece of property. All previous owners (or the heirs of previous owners who have died) must receive notice of the suit. Quiet title suits can take years and cost a lot of money to prepare. The court will distribute the decedent's property according to the laws of intestate succession, discussed in Chapter Four.

Probate in New Mexico can be informal and simple. A routine probate may take less than six months to complete. While some people fear horror stories they have heard about probate, in reality many estates can be probated without spending much time or money. When a person has left a valid will, the personal representative should follow the instructions in the will and distribute the assets to the devisees named in the will. The judge will approve these distributions if the devisees or title companies want a formal closing.

Choosing an Attorney

As in all professions, there are good attorneys and bad attorneys. The public usually only hears about the bad attorneys, but there are many attorneys who are honest, hard-working and competent. As a consumer, you are entitled to choose an attorney who suits your needs. Interview several attorneys and choose the one with whom you think you can best work. Not all attorneys know all kinds of law. Some specialize in criminal law, divorce law, elder law, business law or other areas. Other attorneys do a little of everything. When you seek legal advice, you should first **state what kind of legal problem you have**. If the attorney does that kind of law, you might ask some or all of the following questions before hiring the attorney:

1. What are your hourly rates? (If the attorney or staff will not give this information over the phone, find another attorney.)
2. For my particular problem, do you charge by the hour or a flat fee?
3. Is there a minimum or maximum amount I will be charged?
4. Do you charge a retainer fee? (Most attorneys do.) If so, how much?
5. Do you have a sliding-scale fee for lower income people? (Some attorneys do.)
6. Do you offer an initial free consultation? In person or over the telephone? If so, for how many minutes?
7. How long have you practiced in this area of the law?
8. What is your policy for returning phone calls? Do you return them within the day, one day, one week, etc.?
9. Will I be charged a minimum amount for each phone call, i.e., if we talk for five minutes, will you charge me for 15 minutes?
10. Have you ever been reprimanded, suspended or disbarred? (If the attorney answers yes, this means that the state

Disciplinary Board has ruled that the attorney has done something wrong.)
11.   How long will it take you to do this legal work? A day? A week? A month? Years?

You might ask some of these questions over the telephone. Other questions you might ask during the initial meeting with the attorney. Do not feel pressured into hiring an attorney with whom you do not feel comfortable. If you do decide to use a particular attorney, do not be surprised if the attorney asks you to sign a **fee agreement**. Fee agreements are for both your protection and your attorney's protection and should set out the scope of the work, the attorney fee to be charged, other costs and expenses, provisions for terminating the contract, a time estimate and the attorney's billing procedure.

The Lawyer's Code of Professional Responsibility requires a lawyer to abide by certain rules. Communications between the lawyer and client must be kept **confidential**. The fees charged by the lawyer must be **reasonable**. The lawyer must be **competent** to do the type of work requested.

If you feel you have been the victim of a dishonest attorney, contact the Disciplinary Board of the Supreme Court, 400 Gold SW, Suite 800, Albuquerque, NM 87102, 505-842-5781, and ask for a complaint form to fill out. The Disciplinary Board governs the conduct of all attorneys licensed in New Mexico. Even if the board chooses not to discipline an attorney for a complaint that was filed, the board does investigate every complaint filed.

Unauthorized Practice of Law Prohibited

New Mexico law prohibits the unauthorized practice of law. This means that nonlawyers cannot provide legal assistance, for fees or otherwise. Nonlawyers cannot practice law or hold themselves out to the public as people qualified to practice law. Nonlawyers cannot prepare wills, trusts, powers of attorney, living wills, probate papers, guardianship or conservatorship papers, the affidavits discussed earlier or other legal documents for others. People found guilty of violating this law can be fined up to $500 or be imprisoned for up to six months, or both.

This book is meant to inform the public about issues concerning them. The author hopes the book will answer questions and educate people about New Mexico law. An individual is free to prepare his or her own legal documents (whether this is wise is another question) but may **not** prepare legal documents for others. Paralegals, legal assistants and other legal staff who are supervised by an attorney may assist in preparing legal documents, but the attorney is ultimately responsible for the documents.

☞ **Alzheimer's Association (for NM)**
8100 Mountain Rd. NE, Ste. 102
Albuquerque, NM 87110
505-266-2195

☞ **American Association of Retired Persons (AARP)**
AARP New Mexico
535 Cerrillos Rd., Suite A
Santa Fe, NM 87501
Phone: (505) 820-2277
Email   address:
nmaarp@aarp.org
www.aarp.org

☞ **Bernalillo County Probate Court**
One Civic Plaza NW, 6th Floor
Albuquerque, NM 87102
505-768-4247, 505-768-4028
www.bernco.gov/probate_judge

☞ **Desert State Life Management Services**
(provides financial and personal care assistance for New Mexicans, sliding scale fees charged)
320 Central SW, Suite 200
Albuquerque, NM 87102
505-843-7535

☞ **Disciplinary Board of the Supreme Court**
(check disciplinary record of any New Mexico attorney)
400 Gold SW, Suite 800
Albuquerque, NM 87102
505-842-5781

☞ **EMS Bureau**
(provides information packets with a sample EMS-DNR form and order form for more)
EMS Bureau
New Mexico Department of Health
2500 Cerrillos Rd.
Santa Fe, NM 87505
505-476-7701
www.ipems.com

☞ **Health Insurance and Benefits Assistance Corps (HIBAC Program)**
(trained volunteers counsel seniors on health and long-term care insurance policies and Medicare, free)
2550 Cerrillos Rd.
Santa Fe, NM 87505
1-800-432-2080

☞ **Institute of Public Law**
(packet with values history form and advance health care directive similar to UHCDA form, $3.00)
Institute of Public Law
MSC11 6060
1 University of New Mexico
Albuquerque, NM 87131
505-277-5006
Advance Directive Packets with power of attorney forms may also be available from your local senior centers.

☞ **La Familia**
(a non-profit social service agency licensed to provide care management and support services for adults and also for adolescents)
707 Broadway NE, #103
Albuquerque, NM 87102
505-766-9361 (Albuquerque)
www.la-familia-inc.org

☞ **Lawyer Referral for the Elderly Program**
(free statewide referral service to help seniors with various legal problems find an appropriate attorney for free, reduced fee or payment; also provides information and workshops)
State Bar of New Mexico
P.O. Box 25883
Albuquerque, NM 87125

797-6005 (Albuquerque)
1-800-876-6657 (outside Abq)
www.nmbar.org

☞ **New Mexico Aging and Long-Term Services Department**
(oversees many programs for seniors and administers funds for senior centers and other facilities)
2550 Cerrillos Rd.
Santa Fe, NM 87505
1-800-432-2080

☞ **New Mexico Human Services Department**
(information on adult protective services, income support programs and social services)
P.O. Box 2348
Santa Fe, NM 87504
1-800-432-6217

☞ **New Mexico Insurance Commission**
(regulates and investigates insurance companies doing business in NM)
PERA Building
P.O. Drawer 1269
Santa Fe, NM 87504-1269
505-827-4500 (Santa Fe)
1-800-663-9782 (Public Regulation Commission)

☞ **New Mexico Office of Guardianship**
(information on guardianships and conservatorships; can fund appointment of *guardians ad litem*)
810 W. San Mateo Rd., Ste. C
Santa Fe, NM 87505
1-800-311-2229

☞ **New Mexico State Medicaid Office**
(Medicaid and Nursing Home Benefits questions that your local Human Services Department office cannot answer)
Medical Assistance Division
Human Services Department
P.O. Box 2348
Santa Fe, NM 87504
505-827-3100 (Santa Fe)

☞ **Ombudsman Program**
(advocates for nursing home residents)
2550 Cerrillos Rd.
Santa Fe, NM 87505
1-800-432-2080

☞ **Senior Citizens Law Office**
(free selected legal services to Bernalillo County seniors over age 60; also offers monthly workshops on Medicaid nursing home benefits program and other topics)
4317 Lead Ave. SE
Albuquerque, NM 87108
505-265-2300

☞ **Vital Records**
(copies of birth certificates $10 each, death certificates $5 each; send name, address, birth date, date of death [if applicable], social security number and place of birth or death of the person for whom you need the certificate, your legal relationship to the person, the reason for needing the certificate. Sign and date your request and send it with the required fee to:)
NM Department of Health
Vital Records
P.O. Box 26110
Santa Fe, NM 87502-6110
505-827-2338
www.vitalrec.com/nm.html

☎ Toll Free Numbers and Web Sites

AARP, **www.aarp.org**...1-888-687-2277
Alzheimer's Association (National), **www.alz.org**.......1-800-272-3900
Attorney General (New Mexico), **www.ago.state.nm.us**
    Consumer Protection Division.............................1-800-678-1508
Better Hearing Institute, **www.betterhearing.org**.......1-800-327-9355
Cancer Information Service, **www.nih.gov**..................1-800-422-6237
HIBAC Program (insurance and benefits assistance to NM seniors;
also New Mexico Aging and Long-Term Services Department
number) 1-800-432-2080
Human Services Department (New Mexico) 1-800-432-6217
    www.state.nm.us/hsd
Internal Revenue Service, **www.irs.gov**.............1-800-829-1040 (info)
....1-800-829-3676 (forms only)
Medicare Hotline, **www.medicare.gov**........................1-800-633-4227
Motor Vehicles Division (MVD),
www.state.nm.us/tax/mvd/mvd_home.htm...........1-888-683-4636
New Mexico Legislature, **www.legis.state.nm.us**
New Mexico Salud Managed Care (New Mexikids and Medicaid
info)
    www.state.nm.us/hsd/mad/Index.html 1-888-997-2583
New Mexico State Judiciary,.............................. **www.nmcourts.com**
New Mexico Taxation & Revenue Department, **www.state.nm.us/tax**
Public Regulation Commission (PRC), **www.nmprc.state.nm.us/**.......
....1-800-663-9782
Secretary of State (New Mexico), **web.state.nm.us** 1-800-477-3632
Social Security Administration, **www.ssa.gov** 1-800-772-1213
New Mexico Aging and Long-Term Services Department (New
Mexico) 1-800-432-2080
State Bar of New Mexico, **www.nmbar.org**
    Lawyer Referral for the Elderly Project.................1-800-876-6657
    General Information...1-800-876-6227
Veteran's Administration, **www.va.gov** 1-800-827-1000

The six forms in Appendix 2 may be copied without the author's permission.

Do not use these forms if you do not understand them. Consult an attorney of your choice if you have questions (*see* the Epilogue on page 211 for information on selecting an attorney).

These forms are also available from our website:
www.abogadapress.com

Some of these forms may be found in office supply stores.

Form 1 — New Mexico Power of Attorney, page 220
Power of Attorney Form discussed on page 7

Form 2 — Values History Form, page 226
Values History Form discussed on page 11

Form 3 — Health Care Directives, page 234
Health Care Directives discussed on page 36

Form 4 — Cremation Authorization Form, page 242
Cremation Form discussed on page 125

Form 5 — Affidavit of Successor in Interest, page 243
Affidavit discussed on page 203

Form 6 — Affidavit of Homestead Transfer, page 245
Affidavit discussed on page 204

Form 1—New Mexico Power of Attorney

(**NOTE:** The following power of attorney form is allowed by New Mexico law and is provided for your information. You are not required to use this form. **This form may not be appropriate for individuals with complex estates.** The Internal Revenue Service may not honor this form. Do not sign the form if you do not understand it. Consult an attorney of your choice if you have questions.)

THE POWERS GRANTED BY THIS DOCUMENT ARE BROAD AND SWEEPING. THIS FORM, THE NEW MEXICO STATUTORY SHORT FORM UNDER SECTION 45-5-501 NMSA 1978, DOES NOT PROHIBIT THE USE OF ANY OTHER FORM.

POWER OF ATTORNEY
(New Mexico Statutory Short Form)

I, _____(name), reside in _____(city), _____ County, New Mexico. I appoint _____ (name(s)) and relationship(s)) to serve as my attorney(s)-in-fact.

If any attorney-in-fact appointed above is unable to serve, then I appoint _____(name and relationship) to serve as successor attorney-in-fact in place of the person who is unable to serve.

This power of attorney shall not be affected by my incapacity but will terminate upon my death unless I have revoked it prior to my death. I intend by this power of attorney to avoid a court-supervised guardianship or conservatorship. Should my attempt be defeated, I ask that my agent be appointed as guardian or conservator of my person or estate.

CHECK AND INITIAL THE FOLLOWING PARAGRAPH **ONLY IF** YOU WANT YOUR ATTORNEY(S)-IN-FACT TO BE ABLE TO ACT ALONE AND INDEPENDENTLY OF EACH OTHER. IF YOU DO NOT CHECK AND INITIAL THE FOLLOWING PARAGRAPH AND MORE THAN ONE PERSON IS NAMED TO ACT ON YOUR BEHALF THEN THEY MUST ACT JOINTLY.

❏
[   ]
Initials

If more than one person is appointed to serve as my attorneys-in-fact then they may act severally, alone and independently of each other.

My attorney(s)-in-fact shall have the power to act in my name, place and stead in any way which I myself could do with respect to the following matters to the extent permitted by law:

INITIAL IN THE OPPOSITE BOX EACH AUTHORIZATION WHICH YOU DESIRE TO GIVE TO YOUR ATTORNEY(S)-IN-FACT. YOUR ATTORNEY(S)-IN-FACT SHALL BE AUTHORIZED TO ENGAGE ONLY IN THOSE ACTIVITIES WHICH ARE INITIALED.

1. real estate transactions; .... [   ]
2. stock and bond transactions; .... [   ]
3. commodity and option transactions; .... [   ]
4. tangible personal property transactions; .... [   ]
5. banking and other financial institution transactions; .... [   ]
6. business operating transactions; .... [   ]
7. insurance and annuity transactions; .... [   ]
8. estate, trust and other beneficiary transactions; .... [   ]
9. claims and litigation .... [   ]
10. personal and family maintenance; .... [   ]

11. benefits from social security, medicare, medicaid or other government programs or civil or military service; .... [ ]
12. retirement plan transactions; .... [ ]
13. tax matters, including any transactions with the Internal Revenue Service; .... [ ]
14. decisions regarding lifesaving and life prolonging medical treatment; .... [ ]
15. decisions relating to medical treatment, surgical treatment, nursing care, medication, hospitalization, institutionalization in a nursing home or other facility and home health care; .... [ ]
16. transfer of property or income as a gift to the principal's spouse for the purpose of qualifying the principal for governmental medical assistance; .... [ ]
17. ALL OF THE ABOVE POWERS, INCLUDING FINANCIAL AND HEALTH CARE DECISIONS. IF YOU INITIAL THE BOX ON LINE 17, YOU NEED NOT INITIAL ANY OTHER LINES; .... [ ]

SPECIAL INSTRUCTIONS:
ON THE FOLLOWING LINES YOU MAY GIVE SPECIAL INSTRUCTIONS LIMITING OR EXTENDING THE POWERS YOU HAVE GRANTED TO YOUR AGENT.

_____

_____

CHECK AND INITIAL THE FOLLOWING PARAGRAPH IF YOU INTEND FOR THIS POWER OF ATTORNEY TO BECOME EFFECTIVE **ONLY IF** YOU BECOME INCAPACITATED. YOUR FAILURE TO DO SO WILL MEAN THAT YOUR ATTORNEY(S)-IN-FACT ARE EMPOWERED TO ACT ON YOUR BEHALF FROM THE TIME YOU SIGN THIS DOCUMENT UNTIL YOUR DEATH UNLESS YOU REVOKE THE POWER BEFORE YOUR DEATH.

❏
[ ]
Initials

This power of attorney shall become effective only if I become incapacitated. My attorney(s)-in-fact shall be entitled to rely on notarized statements from two qualified health care professionals, one of whom shall be a physician, as to my incapacity. By incapacity I mean that among other things, I am unable to effectively manage my personal care, property or financial affairs.

This power of attorney will not be affected by lapse of time. I agree that any third party who receives a copy of this power of attorney may act under it.

_____

(signature of principal)

_____

(Optional, but preferred: Your social security number)

Dated: _____, 200__

ACKNOWLEDGMENT

NOTICE: IF THIS POWER OF ATTORNEY AFFECTS REAL ESTATE, IT MUST BE RECORDED IN THE OFFICE OF THE COUNTY CLERK IN EACH COUNTY WHERE THE REAL ESTATE IS LOCATED.

STATE OF NEW MEXICO)
) ss.
COUNTY OF _____)

The foregoing instrument was acknowledged before me this _____ day of _____, 200__, by _____(name of principal).

_____
Notary Public
My Commission Expires:
(Notary Seal or Stamp)

BY ACCEPTING OR ACTING UNDER THE POWER OF ATTORNEY, YOUR AGENT ASSUMES THE FIDUCIARY AND OTHER LEGAL RESPONSIBILITIES OF AN AGENT ACTING ON YOUR BEHALF.

[Most businesses do not currently require the following Affidavit to be filled out by the agent, but they could require the Affidavit in the future. State law includes this Affidavit in the do-it-yourself power of attorney form.]

THIS AFFIDAVIT IS FOR THE USE OF YOUR ATTORNEY(S)-IN-FACT IF EVER YOUR ATTORNEY(S)-IN-FACT ACTS ON YOUR BEHALF UNDER YOUR WRITTEN POWER OF ATTORNEY.

AFFIDAVIT AS TO POWER OF ATTORNEY BEING IN FULL FORCE

STATE OF NEW MEXICO)
) ss.
COUNTY OF _____)

     I/we _____ being duly sworn, state:

     1. _____ ("Principal") of _____ County, New Mexico, signed a written

Power of Attorney on _____, 200__, appointing the undersigned as his/her attorney(s)-in-fact. (A true copy of the power of attorney is attached hereto and incorporated herein.)

2. As attorney(s)-in-fact and under and by virtue of the Power of Attorney, I/we have this date executed the following described instrument: _____

3. At the time of executing the above described instrument I/we had no actual knowledge or actual notice of revocation or termination of the Power of Attorney by death or otherwise, or notice of any facts indicating the same.

4. I/we represent that the principal is now alive; has not, at any time, revoked or repudiated the power of attorney; and the power of attorney still is in full force and effect.

5. I/we make this affidavit for the purpose of inducing _____ to accept delivery of the above described instrument, as executed by me/us in my/our capacity of attorney(s)-in-fact for the Principal.

_____,
Attorney-in-fact

_____,
Attorney-in-fact

Sworn   to   before   me   by
_____ this _____ day of
_____, 200__ .

_____
Notary Public

My commission expires:

(notary seal or stamp)

Form 2—Values History Form

Indicate your name and the date.   _____

_____

If someone assisted you in completing this form, please give their name, address and relationship to you.   _____

_____

The purpose of this form is to assist you in thinking about and writing down what is important to you about your health. If you should at some time become unable to make health care decisions for yourself, your thoughts as expressed on this form may help others make a decision for you in accordance with what you would have chosen.

The first section of this form asks whether you have already expressed your wishes concerning medical treatment through either written or oral communications and if not, whether you would like to do so now. The second section of this form provides an opportunity for you to discuss your values, wishes and preferences in a number of different areas, such as your personal relationships, your overall attitude toward life and your thoughts about illness.

SECTION 1

A. WRITTEN LEGAL DOCUMENTS

Have you written any of the following legal documents? If so, for each, please give the date written and the document location, in addition to the other requested information.

End-of-Life Decisions. Are there any limitations, special requests, etc.?
Durable Power of Attorney. Whom have you named to be your decision-maker?

Durable Power of Attorney for Health Care Decisions. Whom have you named to be your decision-maker?

Organ Donations. Are there any limitations on which organs you would like to donate?

B. WISHES CONCERNING SPECIFIC MEDICAL PROCEDURES

If you have ever expressed your wishes, either written or orally, concerning any of the following medical procedures, please complete the requested information. If you have not previously indicated your wishes on these procedures and would like to do so now, please complete this information. For each procedure, indicate to whom you expressed your wishes and when you did so, whether orally or in writing. If in writing, please indicate the document location.

Organ Donation.

Kidney Dialysis.

Cardiopulmonary Resuscitation (CPR).

Respirators.

Artificial Nutrition.

Artificial Hydration.

C. GENERAL COMMENTS

Do you wish to make any general comments about the information you provided in this section?

SECTION 2

A. YOUR OVERALL ATTITUDE TOWARD YOUR HEALTH

1. How would you describe your current health status? If you currently have any medical problems, how would you describe them.

2. If you have current medical problems, in what ways, if any, do they affect your ability to function?

3. How do you feel about your current health status?

4. How well are you able to meet the basic necessities of life— eating, food preparation, sleeping, personal hygiene, etc.?

5. Do you wish to make any general comments about your overall health?

B. YOUR PERCEPTION OF THE ROLE OF YOUR DOCTOR AND OTHER HEALTH CAREGIVERS

1. Do you like your doctors?

2. Do you trust your doctors?

3. Do you think your doctors should make the final decision concerning any treatment you might need?

4. How do you relate to your caregivers, including nurses, therapists, chaplains, social workers, etc?

5. Do you wish to make any general comments about your doctor and other health caregivers?

C. YOUR THOUGHTS ABOUT INDEPENDENCE AND CONTROL

1. How important is independence and self-sufficiency in your life?

2. If you were to experience decreased physical and mental abilities, how would that affect your attitude toward independence and self-sufficiency?

3. Do you wish to make any general comments about the value of independence and control in your life?

D. YOUR PERSONAL RELATIONSHIPS

1. Do you expect that your friends, family and/or others will support your decisions regarding medical treatment you may need now or in the future?

2. Have you made any arrangements for your family or friends to make medical treatment decisions on your behalf? If so, who has agreed to make decisions for you and in what circumstances?

3. What, if any, unfinished business from the past are you concerned about (e.g., personal and family relationships, business and legal matters)?

4. What role do your friends and family play in your life?

5. Do you wish to make any general comments about the personal relationships in your life?

E. YOUR OVERALL ATTITUDE TOWARD LIFE

1. What activities do you enjoy (e.g., hobbies, watching TV, etc.)?

2. Are you happy to be alive?

3. Do you feel that life is worth living?

4. How satisfied are you with what you have achieved in your life?

5. What makes you laugh or cry?

6. What do you fear most? What frightens or upsets you?

7. What goals do you have for the future?

8. Do you wish to make any general comments about your attitude toward life?

F. YOUR ATTITUDE TOWARD ILLNESS, DYING AND DEATH

1. What will be important to you when you are dying (e.g., physical comfort, no pain, family members present, etc.)?

2. Where would you prefer to die?

3. What is your attitude toward death?

4. How do you feel about the use of life-sustaining measures in the face of:
   terminal illness?
   permanent coma?
   irreversible chronic illness (e.g., Alzheimer's disease)?

5. Do you wish to make any general comments about your attitude toward illness, dying and death?

G. YOUR RELIGIOUS BACKGROUND AND BELIEFS

1. What is your religious background?

2. How do your religious beliefs affect your attitude toward serious or terminal illness?

3. Does your attitude toward death find support in your religion?

4. How does your faith community, church or synagogue view the role of prayer or religious sacraments in an illness?

5. Do you wish to make any general comments about your religious background and beliefs?

H. YOUR LIVING ENVIRONMENT

1. What has been your living situation over the last 10 years (e.g., lived alone, lived with others, etc.)?

2. How difficult is it for you to maintain the kind of environment for yourself that you find comfortable? Does any illness or medical problem you have now mean that it will be harder in the future?

3. Do you wish to make any general comments about your living environment?

I. YOUR ATTITUDE CONCERNING YOUR FINANCES

1. How much do you worry about having enough money to provide for your care?

2. Would you prefer to spend less money on your care so that more money can be saved for the benefit of your relatives and/or friends?

3. Do you wish to make any general comments concerning your finances and the cost of health care?

J. YOUR WISHES CONCERNING YOUR FUNERAL

1. What are your wishes concerning your funeral and burial or cremation?

2. Have you made your funeral arrangements? If so, with whom?

3. Do you wish to make any general comments about how you would like your funeral and burial or cremation to be arranged or conducted?

K. OPTIONAL QUESTIONS

1. How would you like your obituary (announcement of your death) to read?

2. Write yourself a brief eulogy (a statement about yourself to be read at your funeral).

SUGGESTIONS FOR USE
After you have completed this form, you may wish to provide copies to your doctors and other health caregivers, your family, your friends, and your attorney. If you have an End-of-Life Directive or Durable Power of Attorney for Health Care Decisions, you may wish to attach a copy of this form to those documents.

For more information, contact:
UNM HSC Institute for Ethics
MSC11 6095
1 University of New Mexico
Albuquerque, NM 87131-0001
Telephone: 505-272-4566 or 505-272-0552
E-mail: **ethics@salud.unm.edu**
http://hsc.unm.edu/ethics/

The Ethics Program provides copies of the Values History Form in booklets for a small fee.

Form 3—Optional Form, Combined Health Care Power of Attorney and Health Care Instructions

This form is similar, but not identical, to the form included in New Mexico's Uniform Health-Care Decisions Act.

OPTIONAL ADVANCE HEALTH CARE DIRECTIVE

This form lets you give instructions about your own health care and/or name someone else (an agent) to make health care decisions for you if you become unable to make your own decisions. You may fill out some or all of this form. You may change all or any part of it, or use a different form. If you have already signed a durable power of attorney for health care and/or a right to die statement (living will), these are still valid. If you wish to combine the health care instructions found in these documents, you may use this optional form.

If you do fill out this form, be sure to sign and date it. You have the right to revoke (cancel) or replace this form at any time. Give copies of this signed form to your health care providers and institutions, any health care agents you name, and your family and friends.

THIS FORM IS OPTIONAL. You do not have to use any form; instead, you may tell your doctor who you want to make health care decisions for you. If you have not signed a form or told your doctor who you want to make your health care decisions, New Mexico law allows these people, in the following order, to make your health care decisions (if these people are reasonably available): 1) spouse, 2) significant other, 3) adult child, 4) parent, 5) adult brother or sister, 6) grandparent, 7) close friend.

****

*You may name another person as your agent to make health care decisions for you if you become incapable of making your own decisions. This is called a **durable power of attorney for health care**. You should talk to the person you name as agent to make sure he or she understands your wishes and is willing to act as your agent. You may also name alternative agents if your first choice cannot or will not make health care decisions for you. Unless related to you, your agent may **NOT** be an owner, operator or employee of a health care institution at which you are receiving care.*

This form has a place for you to limit the authority of your agent. If you do not limit your agent's authority, your agent may make <u>all</u> health care decisions for you.

(1) DESIGNATION OF AGENT: I appoint the following person as my agent to make health care decisions for me:

_____

(*name of agent*)

_____

(*address*)

_____

(*city*)   (*state*)   (*zip code*)

_____

(*home phone*)   (*work phone*)

If I revoke my agent's authority or if my agent cannot or will not make a health care decision for me, then I appoint these persons as my alternative agents, to serve in the following order:

_____

(name of first alternative agent)

_____

(address)

_____

(city)   *(state)*   *(zip code)*

_____

(home phone)   *(work phone)*

_____

(name of second alternative agent)

_____

(address)

_____

(city)   *(state)*   *(zip code)*

_____

(home phone)   *(work phone)*

(2) AGENT'S AUTHORITY: My agent is authorized to obtain and review medical records, reports and information about me. My agent is authorized to make all health care decisions for me, including decisions to provide, withhold or withdraw artificial nutrition, hydration and all other forms of health care to keep me alive, except as I state here:

(Add additional pages if needed)

If you do not limit your agent's authority, your agent will have the right to make your health care decisions including:
  (1) selection and discharge of health care providers and institutions;
  (2) approval or disapproval of diagnostic tests, surgical procedures, programs of medication and orders not to resuscitate;
  (3) directions relating to life-sustaining treatment, including withholding or withdrawing life-sustaining treatment and the termination of life support; and
  (4) directions to provide, withhold or withdraw artificial nutrition and hydration and all other forms of health care.

(3) AGENT'S RESPONSIBILITY: My agent shall make health care decisions for me based on this durable power of attorney for health care, any specific health care instructions I give and my other wishes to the extent known to my agent. If my wishes are unknown and cannot be determined, my agent shall make health care decisions for me based on my best interest. In determining my best interest, my agent shall consider my personal values to the extent known.

(4) WHEN AGENT'S AUTHORITY BECOMES EFFECTIVE: My agent's authority becomes effective when my primary physician and one other qualified health care professional determine that I lack the capacity to make and communicate my own health care decisions.

(5) DURABILITY: This durable power of attorney for health care shall remain in effect despite my later incapacity. This power of attorney remains in effect from the date it was signed unless I revoke it or die.

(6) END-OF-LIFE DECISIONS: If I am unable to make or communicate decisions regarding my health care, and **IF**: (I) I have an incurable and irreversible condition that will result in my death within a relatively short time; OR (ii) I become unconscious and, to a reasonable degree of medical certainty, I will not regain consciousness, OR (iii) the likely risks and burdens of treatment would outweigh the expected benefits, **THEN** I direct that my health care providers and others involved in my care provide, withhold or withdraw treatment in accordance with the choice I have initialed below in *one* of the following three boxes:

Initial only ***one*** *box*

[   ]   **(a) I Choose To Prolong Life**: I want my life to be prolonged as long as possible within the limits of generally accepted health care standards. *OR*

[   ]   **(b) I Choose NOT To Prolong Life**: I do not want my life to be prolonged. *OR*

[   ]   **(c) I Choose To Let My Agent Decide**: My agent under my power of attorney for health care may make life-sustaining treatment decisions for me.

(7)ARTIFICIAL NUTRITION AND HYDRATION: If I have chosen above "NOT To Prolong Life", I also specify by marking my initials below:

*Initial your choice in these box*es

[   ]   **I DO Want Artificial Nutrition** *OR*

[   ]   **I DO NOT WANT Artificial Nutrition.**

[   ]   **I DO Want Artificial Hydration** *OR*

[   ]   **I DO NOT Want Artificial Hydration unless required for my comfort.**

(8) RELIEF FROM PAIN: Regardless of the choices I have made in this form and except as I state in the following space, I direct that the best medical care possible to keep me clean, comfortable and free of pain or discomfort be provided at all times so that my dignity is maintained, even if this care hastens my death:

(Add additional pages if needed)

(9) ANATOMICAL GIFT DESIGNATION: Upon my death I specify as marked below whether I choose to make an anatomical gift of all or some of my organs or tissue:

Initial only **one** *box*

[ ] I CHOOSE to make an anatomical gift of all of my organs or tissue to be determined by medical suitability at the time of death, and artificial support may be maintained long enough for organs to be removed.

[ ] I CHOOSE to make a partial anatomical gift of some of my organs or tissue as specified below, and artificial support may be maintained long enough for organs to be removed.

[ ] I REFUSE to make an anatomical gift of any of my organs or tissue.

[ ] I CHOOSE to let my agent decide.

(10) OTHER HEALTH CARE INSTRUCTIONS OR WISHES: *If you wish to write specific instructions about any aspect of your health care and medical treatment, including your end-of-life decisions, you may do so here.* I direct that:

(Add additional pages if needed)

(11)   NOMINATION OF GUARDIAN: I intend by this power of attorney for health care to avoid a court-supervised guardianship. If I need a guardian, I want my agent appointed in this form to be my guardian. If that agent cannot or will not act as my guardian, I want my alternative agents, in the order they are appointed in this form, to be my guardian.

(12)   COPIES OF THIS FORM: A copy of this form has the same effect as the original.

(13)   REVOCATION: I understand that I may revoke this OPTIONAL ADVANCE HEALTH CARE DIRECTIVE at any time, and that if I revoke it, I should promptly notify my doctor, my agent, any health care institution where I am receiving care and any others to whom I have given copies of this document.   I understand that I may revoke the appointment of an agent under my durable power of attorney for health care *(Section 1 of this form)* by a signed writing or by telling my doctor.

SIGN and DATE BELOW:

_____   _____
(your signature)   *(date)*

_____   _____
(print your name)   *(your social security number*
                                 — optional — as verification
_____   *of your identity)*
(address)

_____
(city) (state) (zip code)

(This form does not have to be witnessed to be legally valid. Witnesses are <u>recommended</u> to avoid any concern that this document might be forged, that you were forced to sign it, or that it does not genuinely represent your wishes)

_____   _____
(signature of first witness)   *(signature of second witness)*

_____   _____
(print name of first witness)   *(print name of second witness)*

_____   _____
(date)   *(date)*

_____   _____
(address of first witness)   *(address of second witness)*

[This form complies with the provisions of the *New Mexico Uniform Health Care Decisions Act* of 1995, NMSA 1978 Sections 24-7A-1 to 24-7A-18 (1997 Supp.)]

Form 4—Cremation Authorization Form

On this ____ day of _____, 200__, I, _____ (name), hereby state that upon my death it is my desire to be cremated and that my cremated remains be disposed of in the following manner: *(state where you want your cremated remains scattered/buried)*

_____

Signature of Declarant

This form must be signed above by you and below by <u>either</u> two witnesses <u>or</u> a notary public using the appropriate format that follows.

WITNESSES

We believe the person who signed this document to be of sound mind and under no constraint or undue influence. On this ____ day of _____, 200__, _____(name), of _____ (address), signed this document, consisting of one page, in our sight and presence and declared the same to be his/her cremation wishes, and at his/her request and in his/her sight and presence and in the sight and presence of each other, we signed our names as witnesses.

_____ residing at _____
Witness Signature   Address

_____ residing at _____
Witness Signature   Address

STATE OF NEW MEXICO   )
) ss.
COUNTY OF   _____)

The foregoing instrument was acknowledged before me this ____ day of _____, 200__, by _____(declarant's name).

_____

Notary Public

My Commission Expires:

Form 5—Affidavit of Successor in Interest

Note: The "affiant" is the person or persons swearing to be the successor(s) of the decedent entitled to claim the decedent's personal property. If more than one person is a successor, all must sign this affidavit in the presence of a notary public.

STATE OF NEW MEXICO   )
) ss.
COUNTY OF BERNALILLO   )

AFFIDAVIT OF SUCCESSOR IN INTEREST TO _____
(Name of Decedent)

_____, the affiant herein, having been duly sworn, states upon oath:

    1. The affiant(s) is/are the successor(s) of _____ (name of decedent), deceased.

    2. The value of the entire estate of the decedent, wherever located, less liens and encumbrances, does not exceed $30,000.

    3. Thirty days have elapsed since the death of the decedent. A copy of the death certificate is attached hereto.

    4. No application or petition for the appointment of a personal representative is pending or has been granted in any jurisdiction.

    5. Pursuant to NMSA Section 45-3-1201 (1995 Repl.), the affiant(s), as successor(s) of the decedent, is/are entitled to the payment of any sums of money due and owing to the decedent, to the delivery of all tangible personal property belonging to the decedent and in the possession of another, and to the delivery of all instruments evidencing a debt, obligation, stock or chose in action belonging to the decedent.

DATED: _____, 200___.

_____

AFFIANT*

*each Affiant should sign on a separate line.

_____, Affiant, being first duly sworn, states on oath that all of the representations in this affidavit are true as far as affiant knows or is informed, and that such affidavit is true, accurate and complete to the best of affiant's knowledge and belief.

_____
AFFIANT

      SUBSCRIBED AND SWORN TO before me this _____ day of _____, 200__ by _____.

                        _____
                        NOTARY PUBLIC

My Commission Expires:

Form 6—Affidavit of Homestead Transfer

AFFIDAVIT OF SURVIVING SPOUSE PURSUANT TO SECTION 45-3-1205, NMSA 1978

The undersigned, _____,
(name of surviving spouse, hereinafter "affiant") being first duly sworn, deposes and states that:

1. Six months have elapsed since the death of _____ (name of deceased spouse, hereinafter "decedent") as shown in the certified copy of the death certificate attached hereto.
2. At the time of death of the decedent, affiant and decedent were married and owned their homestead described as:

    (insert legal description of home here)

    as community property.
3. A copy of the deed with the legal description of the homestead is attached hereto.
4. But for the homestead, the decedent's estate is not subject to any judicial probate proceedings in any court.
5. No application or petition for appointment of a personal representative or for admittance of a will to probate is pending or has been granted in any jurisdiction.
6. Funeral expenses, expenses of last illness and all unsecured debts of the decedent have been paid.
7. The affiant is the surviving spouse of the decedent and is entitled to title to the homestead by intestate succession or by devise (if devised under a valid last will of decedent, the original will is attached to the affidavit).
8. No other person has a right to the interest of the decedent in the described property.
9. No federal or state tax is due on the decedent's estate.

10. The property was the homestead of decedent and affiant as defined in Section 45-3-1205 NMSA 1978 and is assessed for property tax purposes for not more than $100,000.

All of which affiant affirms to be true and correct and further acknowledges that any false statement herein may subject affiant to penalties relating to perjury or subornation of perjury.

Dated:

_____

Affiant's Signature

ACKNOWLEDGEMENT

STATE OF NEW MEXICO   )
)ss.
COUNTY OF   )

     This instrument was subscribed, sworn to and acknowledged before me this _____ day of _____, 200__, by _____, Affiant.

_____
NOTARY PUBLIC

My commission expires:

PLEASE NOTE:

Based on what new laws the
New Mexico Legislature
passes, Abogada Press sells
periodic supplements to
Life Planning in New Mexico.

For information about ordering
Life Planning in New Mexico supplements

send a **self-addressed, stamped envelope** to:

Abogada Press
P.O. Box 36011
Albuquerque, NM 87176-6011

or visit our web site at:
www.abogadapress.com

About the Author

photo by Mark Justice Hinton

Merri Rudd has served as Bernalillo County's Probate Judge since 2001. She received her undergraduate degree from Vanderbilt University and has been an attorney since 1986 when she graduated from UNM's School of Law. After clerking for the Honorable William W. Bivins on the New Mexico Court of Appeals, Rudd focused her practice on elder law, addressing the needs of Albuquerque's senior citizens. She worked at the Senior Citizens Law Office (SCLO), which provides selected free legal services to Bernalillo County seniors over 60.

Rudd spent three years compiling and editing the *New Mexico Senior Citizens Handbook*, published by the State Bar of New Mexico in 1989. In September 1989 she received the state bar's Outstanding Contribution award for her work on the *Handbook*. In 1990 the state bar published the *Elder Law Manual*, a training manual for attorneys who work with senior citizens. Rudd co-authored the *Elder Law Manual* with Ellen Leitzer and Patricia McEnearney Stelzner, attorneys and co-directors of SCLO.

In 1993 Rudd, along with attorney Tom Smidt, drafted and advocated the successful passage of a law that ensures an individual's right to choose cremation. Rudd writes a legal column, "Ask the Probate Judge," for the *Albuquerque Journal's Business Outlook* section. Rudd wrote a legal column for twelve years for *Prime Time* newspaper, which received the State Bar's 1998 Silver Gavel Award and the 1999 North American Mature Publishers Association's Best Entry in Editorial Category award.

Rudd closed her private law practice in 1997, but contributes to the elder law field. Ms. Rudd has taught wills, trusts, and probate at TVI and has served as an adjunct professor at the UNM Law School. She owns Abogada Press, which publishes books about law for the public. In addition to *Life Planning in New Mexico*, Abogada Press also published *Family Law in New Mexico* by Barbara L. Shapiro in 1998.

In her spare time Rudd enjoys raising native wildflowers, hiking, swimming, cross country skiing, baking, contra dance calling, and volunteering in the community.

❖ ❖ ❖

Order Form		
Please send me the book *Life Planning in New Mexico*		
Name		
Address		
City, ST Zip		
Phone #		
Quantity	Price	Total
	$19.95 (single copy)	
	$18.95 each (2 to 5 books)	
	$17.95 each (6 to 15 books)	
	$15.95 each (over 15 books)	
Sales tax: **6.0%** (added to all books shipped to a NM address)		
Shipping: $2.50 for 1st book $1.00 each additional book		
Total enclosed:		
Please send a copy of this form with your check or money order to: ❖Abogada Press PO Box 36011 Albuquerque, NM 87176 *Thank you.*		

Abogada Press has also published the book *Family Law in New Mexico* by Barbara L. Shapiro. This book is a guide to state law on marriage, divorce, property and debt division, child custody and support, spousal support, grandparent rights, and more.

Order Form		
Please send me the book *Family Law in New Mexico*		
Name		
Address		
City, ST Zip		
Phone #		
Quantity	Price	Total
	$18.95 (single copy)	
	$17.95 each (2 to 5 books)	
	$16.95 each (6 to 15 books)	
	$14.95 each (over 15 books)	
Sales tax: **6.0%** (added to all books shipped to a NM address)		
Shipping: $2.50 for 1st book $1.00 each additional book		
Total enclosed:		
Please send a copy of this form with your check or money order to: ❖Abogada Press PO Box 36011 Albuquerque, NM 87176 *Thank you.*		